NIVEN'S
HOLLYWOOD

NIVEN'S HOLLYWOOD

Tom Hutchinson

Introduction by PETER USTINOV
Afterword by DAVID NIVEN Jr

Macmillan

To Pat, my wife

First published 1984 by
MACMILLAN LONDON LIMITED
London and Basingstoke
Associated companies in Auckland, Dallas,
Delhi, Dublin, Hong Kong, Johannesburg, Lagos,
Manzini, Melbourne, Nairobi, New York,
Singapore, Tokyo, Washington and Zaria

This book was designed and produced by
The Rainbird Publishing Group Ltd,
40 Park Street, London W1Y 4DE

ISBN 0 333 37025 2

Picture Research: Tomás Graves
Designer: Lee Griffiths

Text set by SX Composing Ltd, Rayleigh, Essex, England
Photographs originated by Anglia Reproductions, Witham, Essex, England
Printed and bound by Mackays of Chatham Ltd, Kent, England

Previous page: David Niven in the title role as the elegant gentleman burglar in Raffles *(1939).*

Contents

Introduction by Peter Ustinov

I met David Niven under circumstances which would not have favoured a close companionship, let alone friendship, had his personality been other than it was. He was a lieutenant-colonel, and I was a private. The war was on. I was supposed to write a script for him, in collaboration with Major Eric Ambler, for Captain Carol Reed to direct.

In those days, nothing much had changed in the officer-man relationship since Waterloo, and there was no administrative possibility of maintaining an ordinary soldier, 6411623 in my case, in close proximity to an officer unless the one were the orderly of the other. Consequently, for the purpose of writing a screenplay, I became David Niven's batman.

He was quick to sense the anomaly of the situation, and did his best to alleviate the complexes which had taken root in me during basic training. At his insistence, I was given a sleeping-out pass, although even he could not avoid my having to cross the whole of London at dawn in order to parade for breakfast at the Express Dairy at Wembley Park, after which I would have to wash my utensils, and travel all the way back to the Ritz Hotel, where we had our production office. The War Office was willing, albeit grudgingly, to allow an enlisted man to work on a script, but breakfast at the Ritz would have been a dangerous abuse of privilege.

David did what he could to render our collaboration agreeable, to the extent of giving me a pass which stated that 'This man may do anything and go anywhere in the course of his duties, according to his own judgement.'

Stopped one afternoon in the middle of London by a military policeman, I produced this pass. His avid smile faded as he read it, and he exploded with an obscenity not devoid of jealousy. 'Lucky ———,' he muttered.

I told him I was an even luckier ——— than he imagined, since if he looked closely at the signature, he would see that I also had David Niven's autograph.

David's image, to use that frightful word, one of the blights of our times, was that of a cheerful and indomitable optimist, born into a certain class, who knew all about the rough and the smooth and about the thick and the thin and who rolled with the punch only to emerge victorious in the end, without a hair out of place.

He was, of course, all this, but a great deal more as well. Like all those who made jokes about their inherent cowardice, he was a man

A studio portrait of 1937, redolent of the Hollywood notion of an English gentleman — dapper, assured and maybe just a little too smooth.

6

of extraordinary courage, with a caustic and diabolic sense of fun about that very background which had given him his relaxed aristocratic posture.

Naturally he exploited his attributes to the full as a performer. It could be said that he always played different aspects of himself within a fairly narrow range, but later in his career he was quite capable of surprise, as with his Oscar-winning performance in *Separate Tables* (1958). He never tired of referring to himself as immensely lucky, as though he were well paid for an undemanding labour of love, but such grace and modesty were part of his education, and did not entirely reveal the ebullient observer of human folly who hid behind the whimsical and temperate façade.

It was with his writings that he fully came into his own. He was no longer merely the witty, elegant performer of parts which lay within his range, but a chronicler of devastating precision. When the films have relapsed into the shadows owing to changes of fashion, and when even styles of acting become redolent of certain periods of history, the writings will retain their mordancy and their wonderful freshness.

David was indeed more than an actor; he was a rounded person. He was born with an extraordinary clarity of vision about the life style which has engulfed lesser men, relegating them to the status of club bores and waffling caricatures. He relished the surrealism sometimes evident in the very class from which he grew. The general in the Western Desert who sat behind a desk in his tent, upon which were three trays, the one, quite well filled, marked 'In', the second, empty, marked 'Out' and the third, overflowing with papers, marked 'Too Difficult'. On hearing this anecdote from David, one was left with the impression that this General was probably as responsible for the Allied victory as any other.

Another general, marking examination papers at Sandhurst, wrote about a cadet: 'This candidate sets himself remarkably low standards, which he unfortunately fails to live up to.'

David's own Commanding Officer remarked on David's return from Hollywood to resign his commission from the regular army:
C.O.: Good God, Niven, we haven't seen you for a week or two. Where've you been?
NIVEN: In America, sir. Making pictures.
C.O.: Pictures? (A long pause for contemplation) Water colours?

David was adept at being himself in public. He was a dispenser of laughter and of well-being. But perhaps he managed so admirably in this public service because he was no stranger to drama and to sadness. The accidental death of his first wife during a party game, made more horrible by its absurdity, left a mark on his substance if not on the polished patina, and his frantic worry when one of his adopted daughters was involved in a car smash revealed him to be a man capable of the most acute suffering. Despite the frivolity of his

With Peter Ustinov on the set of Lady L (1965), a featherweight period romance originally intended as a vehicle for Tony Curtis, Gina Lollobrigida and Ralph Richardson with George Cukor directing. After a series of wrangles over the script, Ustinov replaced Cukor in the director's chair and Niven, Sophia Loren and Paul Newman stepped into the starring roles. Ustinov and Niven had begun a lifelong friendship during World War II, when they worked together on Carol Reed's The Way Ahead (1944).

youth, the buccaneering spirit he shared with his friends Errol Flynn and Douglas Fairbanks Jr, and despite the fact that he jealously preserved the pleasantly debonair effervescence, he mellowed into a man of much shrewder perceptions, both human and social, than he was usually given credit for. He needed and sought out friendships, which was perhaps the consequence of a taste for the camaraderie germane to the military establishment, but despite his effusiveness, he was one to look facts coolly if not coldly in the face and his judgements were sometimes severe and at no time sentimental.

When he lost his power of sustained speech during his terminal illness, he confided to a friend his conviction that it was a celestial punishment for having talked too much.

It takes more than death to silence such a unique spirit. There remain pictures and, above all, words, to stand in for the soundless voice, and they are enough to ensure his presence among the living for many years to come.

9

Land of Promises

The Hollywood to which David Niven was introduced in 1935 was very different not only from the television-dominated Hollywood of today, but also from the 'hick town' it was in 1911, when the film industry 'discovered' it.

In 1935 it was both a place and a state of mind. It was fact and fantasy, both the spider and the web of dreams it wove. Hollywood is a suburb of Los Angeles, which, at the turn of the century, was nothing more than a village surrounded by groves of citrus trees and farms. What it did have was unspoiled countryside ideal for making Westerns, and a lengthy day of natural light, which was a necessary aid to the slow film used then in photography.

Hollywood was just an agricultural community producing citrus fruit before the movies arrived in 1911. Opposite above: The CBS buildings on Sunset Boulevard and below: The dressing-rooms at First National.

By the mid-thirties it was already the dream factory it was to remain for the next two decades. For millions of people in small towns all over America, a far less mobile America than today's, Hollywood's glamour was perhaps the only way of escape from the daily grind – a once weekly window on a magic world where men were braver, women more beautiful and drama more 'real' than real life.

Of course, it was not just the films themselves but the actors and actresses who captured the imagination. Fan magazines and newspaper gossip columnists recorded and embellished the lives of the stars so that their loves and marriages, their expensive way of life by sun-reflecting swimming pools, became the subject of discussion by stenographers and office clerks across the nation.

The fantasy, like the smog, was pervasive and the scent in the air was sexual. Rarely did the sex become real and sordid, at least as far as outsiders were concerned. In 1921, Fatty Arbuckle's career had been ruined spectacularly by one such scandal. It was as though when

Above: An apprehensive sound technician records the roar of Leo the Lion, trademark of MGM. Its history began with Loew's Inc., an exhibition company which in 1920 acquired Metro Pictures and in 1924 merged with Sam Goldwyn's production company. Goldwyn left to go independent, but in 1925 Louis B. Mayer joined the group and dominated the studio's output. Opposite: The prosaic side of the dream machine; the sound effects department (above) and the statuary and lamp props section at MGM (below).

the dream was betrayed or the curtain became threadbare, Puritan America took delight in grinding the dream it had created into dust.

Never can so much attention have been fixed on one village. It was a real life 'soap opera' and the medium was truly the message. Under this great pressure of public attention, many actors and actresses went to pieces, some literally went mad. As we shall see, what was exceptional about David Niven was that he remained absolutely sane. He never lost his sense of proportion; he never became, as so many did, an egomaniac and, most important of all, he never lost his sense of humour. As he wrote later in astonishment: 'I lived in Hollywood for nearly twenty years without visiting a psychiatrist.' Niven was perhaps unique in being so widely respected, even loved, by Hollywood itself. The secret was probably that he never felt exploited, he never felt he was a 'great actor' who was 'slumming'. He was delighted and amused by Hollywood and always believed himself fortunate to

Above: Location shooting on the Pacific coast.
Opposite: A camera crew get ready for action on the corner of Hollywood Boulevard and Vine Street in 1936. In the early days of the talkies the sound track consisted of one reel of film to which no other sounds could be added. This destroyed the flexibility of film making until the introduction, in 1932, of 'mixing', which combined a number of different sound tracks on one track.

Left: A gala première of An American Tragedy *(1931), an adaptation of Theodore Dreiser's tale of the idle rich directed by Josef von Sternberg and starring Phillips Holmes and Sylvia Sidney. The crowd hysteria which underlay these events was brilliantly caught in the climactic scenes of Nathanael West's novel* The Day of the Locust, *a savage satire on Hollywood.*
Below: John Gilbert at the pool-side of his Spanish-style mansion, part of which is pictured opposite. Valentino's successor as the silent screen's greatest lover, Gilbert was the most spectacular casualty of the coming of sound.

be paid for doing what came so easily to him. He was 'planned' as a replacement or understudy to Ronald Colman, and though he did indeed share many of Colman's strengths, he quickly developed his own image and acting style. It was typical that he became one of Colman's closest friends and never a bitter rival.

The stars, and those lower down the pecking order, knew and acknowledged themselves to be as contract-trussed as any other member of a factory town. As such their sometimes outrageous indulgences were seen each by the other as pardonable reactions against restraint. As one scriptwriter said: 'Being in Hollywood is like making love to a porcupine – it's a thousand pricks against one.'

Those within might take this cynical view of themselves. To those outside, theirs was a way of life to be envied, imitated, and subjected to a scrutiny as fierce as it was fond. For the stars, like the gods, were supposed to set an example whether they liked it or not.

Hollywood was a hothouse which boasted both vice and virtue in the intense light of public attention. It was a place of violent extremes, of hypocrisy and humanity, of art and fart, of crassness and integrity. Dreams were for sale by the yard or by the mile. Alexander Mackendrick, the British film director, went there to make the *Sweet Smell of Success* (1957)* with Burt Lancaster and decided he

*The date given against film titles indicates, wherever possible, the year the film was shown publicly for the first time. This was not always immediately after a film had been completed as sometimes release was delayed for several months.

would like to see how his film was being edited. He discovered there was a building at the far end of the studio and on the first floor were all the editors of every film being made; when he announced who he was, there was jubilation and a bottle of whisky was produced. 'You see directors didn't usually pay them a visit. It was all very much an assembly line. You did your particular job and that was it. . . .'

'I think I had the best of it there', Niven once told me. 'People now talk about those times as a golden age, forgetting that the studios conveyor-belted films and people. To survive in that atmosphere of cut-throat competition you had to be very tough.

Almost everyone knew everyone in the Hollywood studios. Each knew what the other's business was about, because each person's business depended upon the other's. Clark Gable was famous for knowing who the carpenters were on his films and all about their families, but that was true of many of the stars. And it was not just that they relied upon each other. In a way, everyone in Hollywood believed in the Hollywood legend: that an obscure dancer called Lucille Le Sueur might one day become Joan Crawford. . . . The fan magazines and the film trade's papers kept the gossip and information flowing about the stars and the producers, the deals and the tycoons like the honey-trickle of Parnassus.

A democracy, of course, it was not, not by any standards: a warring oligarchy, perhaps. Hollywood was dominated and controlled by moguls with immense power because they had immense amounts of money. They had wills and indeed whims of iron and held court like the last Roman emperors. The bizarre extravagance of their taste in fashion was deliberate. It was no accident that Cecil B. De Mille, for example, dressed like a dictator. Interestingly in Mussolini's case, it was he who enjoyed dressing like De Mille, not the other way round. They surrounded themselves with yes-men – 'don't say yes until I tell you' is a Darryl F. Zanuck quote – and the slightest insult was punished as an infringement of sacred protocol. The actor George Bancroft, for instance, a big name in the 1930s, became a low-rated character actor because he had slighted one of the bosses at Paramount. He was crushed by indifference.

David Niven himself went against the rules of such games, sometimes unwittingly, more often than not with deliberate ceremony of purpose. 'You mustn't let the buggers get you down,' he said. Thus, his battles with Sam Goldwyn, who had him under contract for many years, had the flavour of an epic struggle. But Niven's delight in flouting restrictions was as much that of the naughty schoolboy defying regulations, which probably explains why he lasted so long and led such a charmed life. 'And sometimes, you know, you didn't know what the damned rules were all about, anyway.'

There is the story told to me by Niven and, at a different time, by Raymond Chandler, which gives it, by the law of averages, some

Above: Cecil B. De Mille, a former actor and cinema's greatest showman, whose energy, vulgarity and extravagance became Hollywood legends. His films are often laced with a generous helping of calculated, and prurient sex – from Mae Marsh cavorting in a skimpy grass skirt in Man's Genesis *(1912) to Claudette Colbert bathing in ass's milk in* The Sign of the Cross *(1932). He is best remembered for his Roman and Biblical epics and his ebullient celebrations of the pioneer days of the West. Opposite: CB's chair was sacrosanct. In the silent days, a young Henry Hathaway (who later became a famous director) was employed to follow De Mille around everywhere with it, even into the sea on location.*

degree of plausibility, of the film producer Jerry Wald, whose tongue outpaced his talents.

Wald, entering the Warner Brothers staff restaurant, the commissary, decided that he now had enough good movies under his belt to sit at the top table along with the Warner brothers themselves, Jack L., Harry, Abe and Sam. The point is that you were *invited* to sit there; you did not just sit there. But Wald, being the brash character that he was, decided to tough it out.

The Warner brothers continued talking, ignoring Wald. 'Sure,' said Jack L., 'people screw you up these days just for the fun of it. We were going to make Jerry Wald head of production, but how can you rely on him, how can you rely on anybody? Remember Darryl Zanuck? Sure, he helped save the studio with that Rin Tin Tin dog, but we made him head of production didn't we? That's how grateful we were. But how grateful was *he*? What did he do? He quit and joined another studio – to compete with us. Very hurtful.'

Cecil B. De Mille lunching on location with Sam Goldwyn whose suit is more appropriate to a board meeting than a picnic.

Surrounded by his family and grandchildren in 1952, De Mille seems to have mellowed a little. In the same year he directed the circus epic to end them all, The Greatest Show on Earth, which starred Betty Hutton, Charlton Heston, Cornel Wilde, Dorothy Lamour, Gloria Grahame and James Stewart.

There was a pause during which you could hear a contract drop.
'Tell you what, let's save ourselves the agony of being walked out on. Let's fire Wald now before he double-crosses us.'

When Jerry Wald arrived back in his office the desk and carpets had already been removed.

Such caprices of attitude were encountered by Niven again and again. That he overcame and survived is part of his remarkable story; that his charm still managed to shine through it all like a watermark makes it even more remarkable.

'I was lucky in that I had many, many friends. And I mean friends, not just acquaintances. Not only did they help me get work, but they were a very present source of comfort.'

In those early days in Hollywood such friends were of pre-eminent importance, especially as they were of the calibre of Clark Gable, Ronald Colman, Marlene Dietrich and, of course, Errol Flynn, who, says Niven, could only be relied upon for his unreliability. . . .

To those who worked and lived there the glitzy glitter of Hollywood was too often the smile on the face of a tiger that had to be ridden for the sake of wealth and success. It could swipe and maul a life, but Niven learned to tickle it under the chin, petting and coaxing it into doing his bidding. By the time he had finished, it was rolling over on its back, begging for more.

Hollywood was, indeed, a very tough, unpredictable place, but James David Graham Niven had known worse. In his early life he had suffered the hardships of the British public school system and, having survived that institution, he was well fitted to survive Hollywood.

Hard Schools

Hollywood may have been a hard school through which to pass with any sort of honour, but Niven had known worse ones; institutions of learning where knowledge was often administered via the seat of the pants in a sort of sadistic osmosis. For he was of that class and breed in England whose parents believe that their offspring are better seen and not heard, better still, not seen at all. So, as soon as it is legally possible, the children are peeled off the parental vine and sent to preparatory school and later to public school, this last being an audacious misnomer because such schools are public only to those who can afford the high fees. The parents can then relax and carry on their social life without fear of unwelcome interruption, knowing that they have made obeisance to the idea of family life while avoiding its reality. Dues of affection had only to be paid on high days and holidays when the schools returned the aforementioned offspring like parcels that had been going the rounds on some postal circuit.

In David Niven's case, his parents consisted of a French mother and a stepfather, Sir Thomas Comyn-Platt, a leading luminary in the British Conservative Party of the time, although little light or love was spared for the young Niven. Niven's real father had gone missing in the Dardanelles in World War I, leaving many debts behind.

Niven was five years old when he and his sister Grizel, who was two years older than him, were told of their father's death. It had no immediate effect on him although, as he grew older, the vacuum created by the absence of a loving father undoubtedly damaged him emotionally. There was an emptiness which Niven hid behind a mask of nonchalance and a courageous gaiety.

Niven was born on 1 March 1910, at Kirriemuir in Scotland, the descendant of two generations of military men. Moving South, after his mother's remarriage to Sir Thomas Comyn-Platt, he was to need all these hereditary martial virtues. He was the youngest child, with an elder brother, Max, who was a naval cadet, and two sisters: Grizel, who was at boarding school, and Joyce, who stayed at home to help her mother. Niven was sent to a boarding school at Worthing.

He later wrote: 'Apart from the Chinese the only people in the world who pack their sons off to the tender care of unknown, often homosexual, schoolmasters at the exact moment when they are most in need of parents' love and influence are the British so-called upper and middle classes.'

So, at the age of six he discovered that 'life could be hell' – a find usually reserved for the later years of human existence. He ran the

The young David Niven in an early role as himself.

gauntlet of bullying and sadistic schoolmasters; he always held one responsible for a stuck-out ear which had been wrenched that way, and for two years his life was unrelieved misery. It culminated in an infection caused by a matron's negligence and his leaving this particular school.

After that, the school of Heatherdown seems to have been bliss by comparison. Though there were snobbish humiliations to endure and a headmaster who could cane, when the occasion demanded it. The occasion demanded it a couple of times, for Niven had decided that one way to make life tolerable among his peers was to be the 'self-appointed jester to the upper classes'.

He let the air out of the bellows of the chapel organ to produce a most lavatorial noise, stole a marrow from the kitchen garden of the girls' school next door for his small garden when his school held a flower show, and then sent some dog-mess to a friend in the school hospital. He was expelled because the matron opened the package instead of the patient for whom it was intended. That incident, and the infection neglected by the previous matron, seemed to set some sort of pattern for David Niven's future life – women were to be his downfalling and his setting-up.

From the comparative happiness of the Heatherdown frying-pan Niven was now placed into a much fiercer fire: a 'school for difficult boys'. This was a three-storey house run by a Commander Bollard and his wife as a kind of Whiptheboys Hall, a place, as Niven said, 'of Dickensian brutality'. He was there only a month, but to a child, time never seems to have a stop; death may not be permanent, but life is. The child does not know that there is a limit, that things change. It was quite clearly horrendous, but in his autobiography Niven seems to raise those eyebrows under that corrugated forehead as though to be totally fair-minded; we are asked to 'consider the possibility that I was a thoroughly poisonous little boy'.

If there was anything toxic about such a child we can see, though, that it was adult poison that had been injected. Blake's vision of childlike innocence is here battered around the head by grown-up violence. Niven suggests that Commander Bollard himself suffered from frustration at the balking of his career. This frustration was unleashed on others who were smaller and at his mercy.

Niven once told me that he related some of this to Humphrey Bogart, whose own pampered though parent-distanced childhood was in stark contrast. 'You had it tough, kid,' Bogart told Niven, 'but why didn't you rebel, break out, cause hell?'

A difficult question to answer for an outsider, but when repression is in the air you breathe and the atmosphere in which you live, how do you know how to rebel, how do you know that your treatment is not the norm? Charles Dickens, for instance, kept secret practically until his death the grievous injury that he felt his mother had

inflicted on him when he was young by sending him to a blacking factory. The heart's wound would bleed into later life; but at the time he did not know that it was wrong to be in such pain, because there was no way of life with which it could be contrasted.

So, too, with David Niven. He says that he came to love and understand his mother in later life, a statement which argues that he certainly could not have done so earlier.

All this juvenile humiliation and hurt probably contributed more than anything else to his ability to survive in Hollywood, for in that society there were obvious parallels with the English preparatory- and public-school systems. The figures of authority he was to confront in Hollywood were as capricious and tyrannical as any schoolmaster.

Despite a spell, after Commander Bollard, at a 'crammers', where they tried to stuff Niven full of facts as though he were a Strasbourg goose, he failed to get in to the Royal Navy as had been his intention. So he was sent to Stowe School, a Johnny-come-lately among public schools, but one which already had a high reputation for integrity, and inspired trust in its pupils. It was a milder, more equable place of education than those to which Niven had become accustomed. Stowe completed his education in life's struggles and prepared him

Opposite: Humphrey Bogart, with his wife Lauren Bacall, on board his yacht Santana, *which he bought from Dick Powell for $55,000. Bogart had endured three unhappy marriages before he fell in love with the nineteen-year old Bacall while they were filming Howard Hawks's* To Have and Have Not *(1944). The film contains the memorable scene in which Bacall tells Bogart, 'If you want anything, just whistle'. Bogart took the advice and married her. Bogart was buried with a small gold whistle in his coffin, placed there by Bacall.*

Left: Bogie's young son Stephen evidently disapproves of the beard his father grew especially for The African Queen *(1951), which won his father a well-deserved Oscar.*

Sam Goldwyn, who launched David Niven's Hollywood career, relaxing at home with his wife Frances. As eleven-year-old Samuel Goldfish he left Poland in 1895, spending four years in England, apprenticed to a blacksmith. He arrived in America in 1899, made money in the glove business and then went into the movies, forming Lasky Feature Plays with his brother-in-law Jesse Lasky and Cecil B. De Mille. He changed his name to Goldwyn in 1916, and after the 1924 Metro-Goldwyn-Mayer merger moved into independent production, releasing through United Artists and later RKO. Like all the great movie moguls, he had a crude opportunistic flair – he was an excellent judge of directors – and his craving for artistic respectability led to spectacularly lavish films like Wuthering Heights (1939). George Bernard Shaw once punctured his pretensions by telling Goldwyn, 'The trouble, Mr Goldwyn, is that you are only interested in art and I am only interested in money'.

admirably for the kind of people he was to meet and mix with in the Hollywood years. All tyrannies are the same; it is only the way we define them that makes them different, and Hollywood's class structure was as rigid as any in the schools that Niven had endured.

There were to be the school bullies in the shape of certain studio bosses such as Harry Cohn, head of Columbia; best chums such as Humphrey Bogart, Frank Sinatra and Ronald Colman; headmaster figures such as producer Edmund Goulding and Sam Goldwyn. There were school cads, who were also chums, such as Errol Flynn. Boarding-schoolboys' first sexual fantasies are dreams of school matrons and those girls, beyond the school pale, who were 'town girls'. There were plenty of those to be found in Hollywood.

Difficult boys, out of kilter with the world they inhabit, will often learn the art of camouflage. To be accepted but licensed to be 'different', even eccentric, it is necessary for them not to keep a low profile but rather to adopt the extrovert role of entertainer.

Since his schooldays, Niven saw himself as a 'jester', but not only that: he adapted himself to whatever milieu he was in. It was, after all, the best way of not being hit overmuch. I once put it to him that he had appeared in some rubbishy films considering what I believed to be his fine dramatic talent. Courteous as always in the face of my impertinence, he put up the argument that he had a wife and two children – later four – to support. Then he shook his head. 'No, perhaps it was just too easy to say "yes", to avoid hassle.'

Sam Goldwyn greets Florenz Ziegfeld in 1929, the year in which the great impresario came to Hollywood to supervise Glorifying the American Girl *(1929). Ziegfeld was broke at the time, having lost his fortune in the Wall Street Crash. He was baled out by his wife Billie Burke. Ziegfeld, who died in 1932, has had four films named after him.*

27

It needs no expert psycho-analyst to trace that trait back to childhood and to realize that there must have been many times as a small boy when he had wanted, above all things, to 'avoid hassle'.

It is often said that an actor is all things to all men, that is the nature of his calling after all. It was natural therefore for Niven to be an actor, and it was really only when he became a star that he had the self confidence to allow his own personality full expression.

To return to Stowe: there was to be a foretaste of the enjoyment to be had from holding forth on a stage when he joined Stowe's Officer Training Corps and appeared in a 'military' revue as a dim-witted major general. As Niven wrote about that O.T.C. experience: 'The harpoon of craving success as a performer was planted deep within me.'

Opposite: Cecil B. De Mille and Ernst Lubitsch, a contrast in styles. Head of Production at Paramount for most of the 1930s, Lubitsch was an adept manipulator of the sophisticated comedy of manners. The 'Lubitsch touch' became synonymous with cynical, urbane entertainments, including Trouble in Paradise *(1932)*, Angel *(1937)*, Ninotchka *(1940) and* To Be or Not to Be *(1942). Niven had a supporting role in Lubitsch's* Bluebeard's Eighth Wife *(1938).*

Left: David Niven at the première of They Were Not Divided *(1951), accompanied by his friend Michael Trubshawe, who had a small part in the film. Trubshawe's screen characters belonged to a vanished world of pink gins and 'wizard prangs'.*

Already planted deep within Niven was a very considerable sex drive, which was more and more evident as he grew older. Fortunately, that was taken care of by a girl he called Nessie, a young prostitute with a heart of gold who seems by his account to have been that ideal combination of mother and whore. If she seems almost too good to be true, remember that Niven wrote about her when he was much older and, perhaps, she 'improved' by sentiment and the passing years. At all events he had reasons to be grateful for her and to her for her much-needed love.

More conventionally he met and fell in love with the actress Ann Todd – sacred and profane loves were always popular with the upper classes – but his real education in life was about to begin at Sandhurst Royal Military College.

Joining the army is rather like entering a monastery: obedience is the first virtue preached, of which the other side of the coin is freedom from responsibility. Authority was something to react *against* if necessary, in the safe and sure knowledge that you would never, unless something really dreadful happened, be excommunicated or disowned. You belonged to something; it might not be a family but it was as near as dammit. From all accounts Niven's mischievousness was given free rein at Sandhurst.

From there he was commissioned in 1929 into the Highland Light Infantry and promptly sent to the port of Valletta in Malta, where the sun of the British Empire, if not quite setting, was sitting uneasily on the horizon; things were not quite as they had been.

Niven's escapades there were really schoolboy japes, more so-phisticated of course but, as before, poking fun at authority. The drinking and the late-night truancies were ways of asserting himself. It was pretty obvious that he did not think much of his fellow officers, but he did make one remarkable friend who was to last him the rest of his life, the moustachioed Trubshawe who was later to appear in some of Niven's films as a kind of lucky mascot. Niven describes him as an 'Elizabethan with a hunting horn' and the sound of happy comradeship echoed loud and clear through their years of friendship.

Despite all the fun and comradeship, Niven became convinced that he and the Army were not compatible. So, in 1932, having overstayed one leave, a crime for which he might have been court-martialled, he sent his colonel a telegram which must be unique in the annals of resignation: 'DEAR COLONEL REQUEST PERMISSION RESIGN COMMIS-SION. LOVE NIVEN.'

The next morning he sailed for Canada. His mother had died, he felt he had no responsibilities and he was offered a return ticket to Quebec by a friend who was travelling there, if Niven could give him his car in exchange. What had he to lose?

David Niven at this time was a young man with all the tastes, manners and disposition of a gentleman. The only thing he lacked was

David Niven with the celebrated hostess Elsa Maxwell at a gala night at the Waldorf Astoria Hotel. Maxwell tried unsuccessfully to find Niven work in the movies when he was a struggling unknown.

money. It is intriguing to note how arbitrarily he changed course. It was as if he were prepared again and again to throw his fate into the wind and whether it blew him to Timbuktu or Canada hardly seemed to matter. Canada had been suggested, so Canada it would be.

His early life had been so hemmed in by rules and disciplines that it was inevitable that he would want to be free, but would find it

31

The young stars of tomorrow had to negotiate a seemingly endless obstacle course of mindless publicity stunts.
Left: Warner Brothers starlets see in the New Year with some rather forced gaiety and below: Archery practice for a pert batch of hopefuls including (fourth from left) a young Susan Hayward, whose career nearly got off to the most spectacular of starts when in 1938 she was tested for the part of Scarlett O'Hara in Gone with the Wind. She made her screen début in the same year in Girls on Probation.

Above: Dance director Le Roy
Prinz shows the girls at
Paramount how it is done. Among
his successes was Warner's
biopic of George M. Cohan,
Yankee Doodle Dandy (1942).
Left: Dolores del Rio (centre)
with a gaggle of 'Baby Wampas'
stars. From 1922 to 1934
WAMPAS (Western Association
of Motion Picture Advertisers)
gave annual certificates of merit
to young starlets. Del Rio was a
'Wampas baby star' in 1926,
along with Joan Crawford and
Janet Gaynor.

difficult to decide how to use his freedom. At the moment, he was happy to do what others wanted. Only later in life was he to initiate action for himself. 'I was', he once said, 'very much a drifter . . . I didn't know what I wanted or, really, where I was going. Of course I had ambition, but it was a formless, vague ambition. I just wanted to *be* somebody.'

So to Quebec and the hospitality of friends. After a severe illness caused by badly-infected tonsils, Niven travelled to New York. He did a little bootlegging for a few weeks until the dreaded anti-alcohol legislation was repealed. Then, with other friends, he tried the legitimate side of the drinks business as a door-to-door salesman for wine merchants, meeting some of the toughest characters that ever Damon Runyon might have written about.

He survived, though he scraped very near to disaster one evening when he decided to treat himself to a spree. He picked up a showgirl

Norma Shearer, queen of the MGM lot in the early 1930s, takes to the water at the Ambassador Hotel, Los Angeles. Photographs displaying the supposedly energetic leisure activities of the stars were very popular with the studios.

who said she had been stood up by her date. The unchivalrous gentleman who had left her in the lurch was, it was reported next day to Niven, a very well-known gangster who could easily take mortal offence if he knew that a 'Limey' was muscling in on one of his females.

It was during this period that, through his gift for making and using useful friends, he first met Elsa Maxwell. It is symptomatic of the time and age that Miss Maxwell should have acquired a remarkable reputation simply as a party-giver for what was becoming known as the International Set, even though it was said that she could ill afford it. In fact her functions, at which the gossips met the gossiped-about, were probably financed by the *nouveaux riches* who wanted introductions to the *anciens riches* and those whose names loomed if not in the headlines at least behind them.

She was a dumpy creature with the sweetest smile, who existed solely by courtesy of snobbery. No great conversationalist herself, she

Left: Rudolph Valentino sporting a beard, a macho corrective to the effeminate image created by films like The Young Rajah *(1922). He was cruelly nicknamed 'The Pink Powder Puff', after a story got around that, at his insistence, a restaurant had installed a face powder dispenser in the men's room.*

Right: James Cagney, one of the new breed of tough, fast-talking, all-American heroes of the early 1930s.

was a Ms Fix-It. Her parties may not have been as elegant as those of the French hostesses of the seventeenth century, to whom she liked to be compared, but what they lacked in *brio* they more than made up for in ostentation.

In the way that homosexuals will become devoted to stars such as Mae West and Judy Garland, who are larger than life, so David Niven was attracted to Elsa Maxwell. Not that he was homosexual, but there was a motherliness about her which appealed to him. She was a kind of Mother Courage of her own particular, artificial situation. Despised by some – Ernest Hemingway ridiculed her – others, such as Noël Coward, applauded her spirit and her ability to make something out of nothing.

When she died in 1963 Noël Coward wrote in his Diaries: 'A great sadness. Poor old Elsa died. Another old friend gone. How glad I am that I went to see her a couple of weeks ago and made her laugh. Poor old duck.'

She had dominated and been part of the party scene which she had helped create and when Niven met her, she took him under her

A reserved young Howard Hughes with Ernst Lubitsch, long before he became the world's most famous recluse, a cross between Citizen Kane and Dr Mabuse. He produced his first film, Two Arabian Nights, *in 1927, gave Jean Harlow her big break in* Hell's Angels *(1930), and in the early 1930s produced* The Front Page *(1931),* Scarface *(1932) and* Bombshell *(1933). Perhaps his most enduring cinematic legacy is the memory of Jane Russell's breasts in* The Outlaw *(1943), hovering over a Puritan Hollywood like twin-storm clouds on the horizon.*

*The artist James Montgomery
Flagg sketches director Ernst
Lubitsch between scenes at MGM.*

capacious wing. Or tried to. He wrote that she said to him: 'Selling
liquor . . . that's no good, no good at all . . . get you nowhere . . . you
should go to Hollywood . . . nobody out there knows how to speak
English except Ronald Colman.

'Next week I'm giving a party for Ernst Lubitsch, just a small
dinner . . . plenty of people are dropping in after the theatre so you
be here . . . and I'll introduce you to Ernst and tell him to do something about it.'

Ernst Lubitsch was a most important director in Hollywood and
this was the first time that Hollywood had been mentioned as a
serious target for Niven. It showed how the place was regarded at
that time, like a gold-rush town, a challenge for any young man with
looks and a knowledge of how the world worked; talent was not even
mentioned. Niven, after all, had other credentials which had very

Catch them young. Hollywood treated its child stars with a cruelly refined mixture of coddling and brutality. Louis B. Mayer pulled out all the stops for the tragic Judy Garland, seen here with Fanny Brice (above left) and at the Ice Follies with her frequent co-star Mickey Rooney (above right). Mayer paid Judy's mother a salary to match that of her daughter's. In return Mrs Gumm kept Judy on her special diet of chicken soup and dexedrine and supervised her gruelling schedule. Later she joined forces with Mayer to arrange Judy's first abortion. It was a child the young star had desperately wanted.
Left: Bonita Granville (left), Judy Garland (right), Tommy Kelly and Sybil Jason.

Above: Freddie Bartholomew,
Mickey Rooney (also left)
and Jackie Cooper enjoy a
watermelon feast at a studio
Christmas party. The English
Bartholomew's brief reign as
Hollywood's pubescent version of
C. Aubrey Smith began with
David Copperfield (1935). After
World War II he went into
television and then advertising.
Jackie Cooper's celebrated ability
to cry at will would have helped
David Niven, who had some
difficulty in summoning up a
tear at Merle Oberon's deathbed
in Wuthering Heights (1939).
Cooper's career petered out in the
late 1930s. He is now a successful
television director.

little at all to do with acting: he had been a soldier and a bootlegger, but the implication was that Hollywood was a magic town where dreams came true. Hadn't they come true for so many who had gone there. . . ?

There were the truck-drivers, who were said to have become overnight stars, the girls 'discovered' by talent scouts. Every month there seemed to be some beauty contest or another, the prize for which was going to be a starring role. You could never pin down such rumours and prove them true or false, they remained more exciting as rumours. Even to those who worked there, Hollywood was a totem for all true believers, a contemporary Arcadia. So it was an obvious equation for Elsa Maxwell to make: Niven equalled Hollywood. How had they lived without each other for so long?

The party for Lubitsch turned out not to be of much immediate use. Niven scarcely met the great man and Elsa Maxwell told him that Lubitsch had said it was not a good time to start in movies. 'So I've thought of something else for you – you should marry a rich wife.' Niven was then making only a few dollars a week; in the cloud-cuckoo-land wherein Elsa Maxwell held court anything was possible.

Myrna Loy lunches with a friend in her MGM dressing-room. The studio's pecking order was reflected in the sumptuousness of its stars' dressing-rooms. At MGM, Marion Davies dispensed hospitality from a luxurious bungalow. When she moved to Warner Brothers, the bungalow was dismantled and transported from Culver City to Burbank.

On the links at the Encino Country Club, reserved exclusively for the use of the stars, their friends and other Hollywood 'nobility'.

In real New York, however, it was necessary to eat, and to eat, Niven had to make money. With some friends he formed The American Pony Express Racing Association, which had to do with polo ponies and the winning of lots of races. Years afterwards Niven was unable to explain what the set-up was designed to achieve, but whatever it was, it probably was not entirely legal.

At last it was time for Niven to go to Hollywood. The first thing he did when he arrived was to fall for the Belzer girls, a delectable quartet of lovelies of whom Gretchen was already a famous movie star. Her acting name was Loretta Young.

David Niven's dreams, fuelled by Elsa Maxwell, were now solely about Hollywood and making it big there. He made his way to the Central Casting Office, which hired extras for the big productions. Outside the building was the stern warning: DON'T TRY TO BECOME AN ACTOR. FOR EVERYONE WE EMPLOY, WE TURN AWAY A THOUSAND.

Niven queued up in the hope that he would be one of those who would be employable. He was not. He had omitted to furnish himself with one very necessary item: a work permit. Despondently he made his way out of the building: WE TURN AWAY A THOUSAND — AND ONE.

Here he was the most junior boy in another school of hard knocks and he had already had a taste of what punishment it could mete out. There were to be consolations, though. The Niven personality would see to that. After all, he had survived all the other gauntlets he had had to wriggle through. What or who could be worse than Commander Bollard? He *had* survived. Oh, how he had survived.

Extra Work

It seems entirely appropriate that David Niven's next attack on Hollywood, at a time when British Empire stories were very much in vogue, should have been aboard that symbol of the might that was Britain: a warship of His Majesty's Navy, HMS *Norfolk*, a County Class cruiser.

The ship was on a goodwill tour around the west coast of Mexico and the United States. Niven spotted it in the bay off Santa Barbara and greeted it like a long-lost friend. Its officers welcomed him in the same cordial way, for he had first met them all when the ship was stationed at Malta and then again at Bermuda and he had quickly become a firm favourite with the ship's company. It was a case of drinks all round. And again? Again. A flush of pink gins went around . . . and around.

When he awoke next morning, he must have wondered for a minute or two if he was hallucinating because, through the port hole, he could see the billowing sails and hear the bellowing orders of an eighteenth-century warship. Pig-tailed seamen scurried about the decks. It was all as real and as unreal as a Hollywood carpenter's shop could possibly make it. . . .

For this was a replica of HMS *Bounty*, on a promotional voyage to publicize the film *Mutiny on the Bounty* (1935). Charles Laughton played the infamous Captain Bligh and Clark Gable the saintly Fletcher Christian.

The film star Robert Montgomery was aboard *Bounty*, not because he had a part in *Mutiny on the Bounty* but because he loved ships and was particularly fascinated by this elaborate re-creation of a British eighteenth-century warship. He and Niven decided to drive back in Montgomery's Bentley to the Metro Goldwyn Mayer studios, a hundred miles away, where *Mutiny on the Bounty* was being made.

There, Niven met Frank Lloyd, the director of the film, and the man who was to be his mentor in Hollywood: Edmund Goulding. Goulding, a short squat man of immense vitality, was, in the current Hollywood jargon, 'hotter than a pistol'. He had, in 1932, made *Grand Hotel* for MGM featuring a cluster of that studio's stars.

He had a reputation, like George Cukor, of being able to direct temperamental women stars with a minimum of fuss, but he was no 'ladies' man' in that other, more licentious, sense. He was married to a woman, now terminally ill, with whom he was deeply in love.

He was looking for 'a new face'. Niven might be able to play the role he had on offer: a drunken, dissolute younger brother. Niven

Left: A screen test of the 1930s, as young hopefuls stand in a circle and submit their profiles to the merciless glare of the studio lights. Stories about screen tests are legion. In 1930 Lionel Barrymore got Clark Gable a screen test at MGM and then nearly scuppered his young friend's career by rigging him out in a Polynesian outfit with a flower behind his ear. Not surprisingly, Irving Thalberg gave him the thumbs down. Below: Charles Laughton surrounded by beautiful studio ladies. Off the set, he preferred the company of young men.

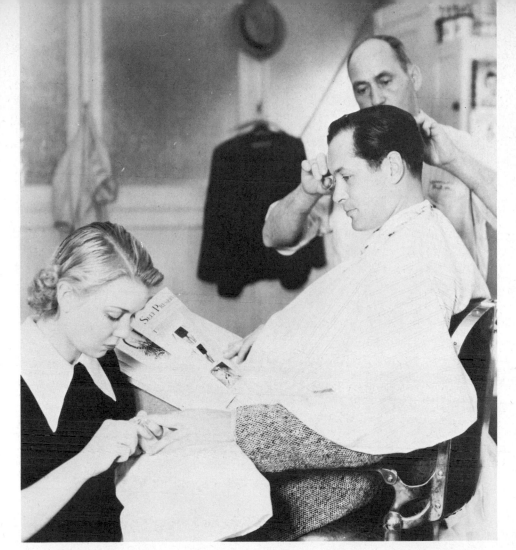

Opposite above: The start of a day in the life of MGM's Robert Montgomery and below: on the set.
Left: A break for a manicure and below: relaxing with a spot of aquaplaning on Lake Norconian. In the 1930s, Montgomery was the studio's all-American playboy and society seducer, steering MGM's glittering leading ladies through a succession of boudoir dramas. Always immaculately groomed, he even wore an evening suit under his flying kit when playing a test pilot in Night Flight (1932).

perked up at that, quipping that he was to the character born, but first there had to be a screen-test. Next day, Niven turned up for the filmed auditions and all he could think of to say was a rude limerick.

The test, as might be expected, was a disaster and Goulding was, by then, too busy really to help his protégé. That help was to come later and Niven was to write about Goulding, 'I owe more to him than to anyone else in the business.'

He hoped he might find a friend at court in the phenomenally busted, sexually charismatic, Mae West. In the interview Niven had with her, she did not speak, but her manager seemed to promise him a role. A few hours later, however, there was a visit from a man from the United States Immigration Service. Niven was now living and working in America illegally. He had to obtain a Resident Alien Visa. Otherwise? The cut-throat gesture did not go unremarked.

Below left: The inimitable Mae West, not the least of whose achievements was to stand conventional sexual morality on its head while continuing to look like a throwback to the 1890s.
Below right: Fitting an exotic hairpiece for the 'Mademoiselle Fifi' sequence in Every Day's A Holiday *(1937), one of her later films muzzled by a new production code which banished her raunchy innuendo from the script.*
Opposite: Photographed by Baron in 1951.

All this for little me? Hollywood gossip columnist Louella Parsons receives a special Academy Award from Cecil B. De Mille. On the left is Darryl F. Zanuck, Vice-President of Twentieth Century-Fox, who began his movie career in the early 1920s writing Rin Tin Tin scenarios. Unlike the noble canine hero, Louella's bite was every bit as unpleasant as her bark. Doubtless both these movie moguls would have preferred to smash the award over Louella's head, but they needed her just as much as she needed them.

Niven went to Mexico – to the town of Mexicali, just beyond the border, where he sat and waited while his birth certificate was sent from England. The bureaucratic process was not to be hurried and, for the moment, even David Niven's resilient spirits seemed to sink.

He eked out his time cleaning guns for the American tourists who came to Mexico to hunt quail. Then, on 1 January 1935, he received his visa and returned to Hollywood. Goulding was out of town, Mae West already had a leading man. Niven did the only thing he could do. He applied at Central Casting again and was told he was 'Anglo-Saxon type No. 2008'. He commented later: 'The first call I got to work as a professional actor was as a Mexican!'

Extras were and are players who are expected to 'fill up' a scene; another name for them was 'atmosphere actors'. There was a seemingly unleapable gulf between them and the principals, those who got to speak, if only a few words. The gap could be bridged, but only rarely. Jane Wyman, born Sarah Jane Faulks, managed to do it and, as an ultimate reward, became Ronald Reagan's first wife. She had had 'bit parts' in Warner Brothers musicals, but her Kewpie-doll face so stood out in a crowd that director Mervyn Le Roy picked her out for a speaking part in *The King and the Chorus Girl* (1937).

That was an exception that proved the rule. 'I knew I was right at the bottom of the heap,' said Niven, 'still I had to start somewhere.' He had tried to get a small part in *Mutiny on the Bounty*, trading on his brief meeting with Frank Lloyd, the film's director, but the latter had other things to worry about. Charles Laughton was being seasick and still looking for an image on which to base his conception of Bligh's character. Laughton always had to do this before getting to grips with a role. It took weeks during the filming of the ill-fated *I, Claudius*, directed by Josef von Sternberg, before Laughton decided that he could use Edward VIII's abdication speech as the basis on which to build his characterization of the Emperor Claudius.

Niven once told me: 'His eventual image of Bligh came to be Frank Lloyd himself. He'd seen Lloyd pacing up and down, looking up with a fierce frown. The only thing he wanted was Frank's . . . eyebrows!'

David Niven knew from the first that an extra's life was not for him. The trek out to location, the way he and his fellows were ordered

Lunching in the studio commissary was a highly class-conscious affair. At MGM Louis B. Mayer had a private dining-room, while the liveliest company was to be found on the 'Directors' Table', whose regulars tossed dice each day to see who would pick up the bill. At Paramount, Cecil B. De Mille's seven-foot-long table, 'The Throne', was placed on a platform above the common herd.

around when they got there, the bad food hurriedly eaten, the general feeling of being completely dispensable was anathema to him. In 1936 only 58 out of 5,500 men extras and 20 out of 6,500 women extras averaged three or more days' work a week. It was a dispiriting existence, humiliating in that the extras available for work hung around the studios like casual stevedores outside a dockyard's gate, hoping for a crumb of employment to be thrown to them.

Niven sat long hours in bars in the hope of meeting useful people and making social contacts. Gradually, he began to be known to assistant directors, who would tip him the wink if there was work going. In addition, he regularly made the rounds of all the studio casting offices and, of course, he did not neglect his social contacts.

At home or in the studio, Douglas Fairbanks Sr was always 'on', the epitomy of ebullient athleticism. Playwright Edward Knoblock, who wrote Kismet *(1930) and* Chu Chin Chow *(1934) and became one of Fairbanks's associates, seems a little alarmed as Fairbanks prepares to swash his buckle all over the Pickfair lawn.*

Niven had met Douglas Fairbanks Sr, the athlete of the movies, playing golf. They met again at the United Artists studio, but were divided by the rigid though unwritten rules that kept the stars from mixing with their 'inferiors'.

Fairbanks was the king of Hollywood, he and his then wife, Mary Pickford, had helped create United Artists, but he was also a jester and it was as a practical joker that he valued Niven's companionship. Sometimes, with the best of intentions, his jokes got Niven into trouble. On one occasion, for example, Fairbanks and Niven were relaxing in a steambath when Fairbanks noticed they had been joined by the all-powerful producer Darryl F. Zanuck. Thinking to boost Niven in Zanuck's eyes, Fairbanks spoke eloquently of Niven's

Douglas Fairbanks Sr and Mary Pickford see Charlie Chaplin off on a trip to Europe.

prowess as a polo player, though why Fairbanks supposed Niven could even play the game let alone excel was not explained. Perhaps it was because polo was so English a game and Niven was affecting, as he put it, 'a very refined accent indeed. It was a sort of self-defence.' Anyway, Zanuck loved polo and his polo parties were social occasions to which only the élite were asked.

It is an indication of how charming and persuasive Niven was then, and always would be, that he was invited. Fairbanks's own public relations technique was also highly persuasive. Niven was called on to play polo at the exclusive Uplifters Club. As Niven wrote later: 'How many two dollars and fifty cents "extras" were getting that break?'

Niven approached it all with his usual air of nonchalance, but, by the end of the day, it was to be severely tarnished. His play was so poor that he became less and less popular with his team, but the worst moment came towards the end of the match. The steed upon which he was mounted took a bite at Zanuck's rear end, a liberty which Zanuck did not find amusing. 'It was', mused Niven, 'a most peculiar way of starting off at the bottom.'

At the bottom Niven most certainly was, but at least now, thanks to Goulding, he had an agent. He was tested with various women stars such as Claudette Colbert, but won none of the parts he had hoped for, often being pipped at the post by Fred MacMurray or Ray Milland. The lottery of Hollywood, however, was about to give him the chance he had almost despaired of.

Irving Thalberg, the undisputed golden boy of Hollywood, creative boss of MGM, married to Norma Shearer, was rumoured to be considering Niven for a part in *Mutiny on the Bounty*.

Rumour or not, Niven was suddenly of interest in Hollywood. Three studios sent representatives to him demanding immediate interviews. Niven had to be sure he accepted the right offer. He did then what he had done before and was to do again. He consulted Edmund Goulding.

Goulding had, in fact, already been extolling Niven's talents to Sam Goldwyn, the most successful independent producer of the moment; but news of other studios' interest in Niven pushed Goldwyn to act. David Niven was summoned to Goldwyn's office and told he was being given a seven-year contract. It was a most unusual offer and Niven could never really explain why Goldwyn had decided to take such a risk with an unknown actor.

At any rate, at the end of a brief interview, Niven walked out of Goldwyn's office a relatively rich man. It seemed, as Goldwyn might have put it, 'he had been included in'.

It would be nice to think that Goldwyn had shrewdly recognized Niven's charm and acting talent, but there were other factors working in Niven's favour. Although Niven believed that one of the reasons for Goldwyn's success was his ability to forget what others were filming and do what he wanted to do, Goldwyn could not ignore the fashion for British-based movies. Anyone who could articulate with what was termed a classy accent was useful. Furthermore, Ronald Colman was about to leave Goldwyn's employ. Although Colman was not really part of the British colony of actors in Hollywood he had a voice and personality with which you could cut glass. His departure meant that Goldwyn needed 'another goddamned Britisher'. David Niven filled that vacant bill more than adequately.

With the seven-year contract Niven had a warning from Goldwyn that no movie would be his until he had learned his craft. That was why he had to 'go out and tell the studios you're under contract to Goldwyn, do anything they offer you, get experience, work hard.' That way he might eventually get a decent part.

It was shrewd advice from one of the shrewdest operators within the Hollywood jungle, an independent tiger who wore nobody's stripes but his own. Being a 'Goldwyn boy' was a promissory note

David Niven accompanies Paramount star Claudette Colbert to the first night of a Hollywood ice revue in 1938. In the early 1930s, Colbert was often cast in sultry roles, notably in De Mille's Cleopatra *(1934), but she was at her best as a brittle comedienne in* It Happened One Night *(1934),* Midnight *(1939), and* Palm Beach Story *(1942). Her temperamental behaviour on the set earned her the tag of 'the Fretting Frog'; she insisted on only being photographed from the left, and on one occasion covered the right side of her face with grease-paint to make her point.*

Above: The 1927 wedding of Norma Shearer and Irving Thalberg, the twenty-eight-year-old 'boy wonder' production supervisor at MGM. By dint of skilful promotion, Thalberg transformed his wife into the epitome of Hollywood glamour and the First Lady of the Screen. Her career faltered after his death in 1936 and she was gradually squeezed out by the studio. Her last film was the 1942 Her Cardboard Lover.

Left: A game of ping pong which seems to have left Thalberg rooted to the spot.

Opposite above and below left: At work, and right: At play.

in itself; even if it was, Goldwyn considered, up to other people to redeem it. A contract was virtually legal tender; it was real estate on paper. It was, most important of all, status.

It is instructive to remember the sort of salaries enjoyed in the film industry in 1935. In that year David Niven earned a meagre $5,200. Goldwyn himself earned $127,500, only just short of Irving Thalberg's $151,762, which itself was less than executive Spyros Skouras's $189,000, while another executive, Nicholas Schenck, laid away $193,434. Mae West earned $480,000, which made her the highest paid woman in the United States at that time.

It was the gossip about money rather than the money itself which mattered most in Hollywood and determined one's place in the hierarchy. The cash was regarded in the light of good-conduct points, such as those awarded in Niven's schooldays.

Niven was always aware of how important it was to make a good impression. He and Cary Grant had once discussed this very point. Grant said that, when he was a small boy called Archibald Leach and was living in Bristol in England, he had early realized that one very good suit was worth three inferior ones. 'Because even when you could see your arse through the trousers of the good suit it still looked

David Niven and three famous members of Hollywood's British community. (Left to right) Brian Aherne, Ronald Colman and Nigel Bruce, who is best remembered as Dr Watson to Basil Rathbone's Sherlock Holmes.

as though it had *been* good.' Archie's father was a tailor's presser and no doubt this helped him preserve his one good suit.

David Niven did his best, too. He showed off his new Ford car, driving speedily around the Hollywood boulevards. Better still, he joined the Hollywood Cricket Club.

The 'British' period of movies in Hollywood was both reflective and prophetic. Films such as *Mutiny on the Bounty*, *David Copperfield* (1935) and *Lloyds of London* (1935) were evidence of an American interest in, and respect for, things British. For although Britain was still accounted an empire, Hollywood sensed that the time of that empire was fast running out. There was glamour and nostalgia to be squeezed from Britain's history and even lessons to be learned. One day soon, America was to have an empire and it needed a morality to justify it.

To make these forays into British history credible, it was necessary, or at least desirable, to have minor parts played by actors with English accents, even if the lead roles had to be played by a big American star such as Gary Cooper in *Lives of a Bengal Lancer* (1935).

Actors such as the eagle-browed C. Aubrey Smith, Henry Stephenson and Nigel Bruce (famed as Dr Watson to Basil Rathbone's Sherlock Holmes) formed the hard core of what developed into a British colony in Hollywood. Basil Rathbone, Herbert Marshall, Ronald Colman and Reginald Gardiner were associated with the colony, yet not of it. They were clubbable when they felt like it, but, perhaps feeling that there had been enough team spirit during their

Above left: Ronald Colman, whose dark good looks armed him for a career as a swashbuckler in the 1920s. With the coming of sound, his soft voice and perfect manners transformed him into the Hollywood incarnation of the romantic Englishman. He became a star at the comparatively late age of thirty-two in The White Sister *(1923), and nearly twenty years later his tact, timing and wry humour were still enthralling female audiences in* Random Harvest *(1943).*
Above right: Colman, Clive Brook and Herbert Marshall, who was a successful leading man at Paramount in the 1930s, despite having lost a leg in World War I. Paramount had intended to promote him as a Great Lover, but he carved a niche in discreet gentlemanly roles opposite powerful leading ladies. The sets in his films had to be designed to conceal his limp.

English schooldays, did not identify themselves totally with the English as a group.

David Niven was also wary about being too obviously of the British colony. Nevertheless, because of all the loneliness and loveless-ness of so many educational institutions, he did need the support of some sort of family. When he found one, as with the army, he would sink into it. What it did give him was a sounding board for his own personality, a structure to react against.

Niven's first Hollywood family was the Hollywood Cricket Club, although unlike some of his English friends he was not obsessed by it. Boris Karloff, the star of so many great horror movies, whose real name was William Pratt, had been born in England and was devoted to cricket. Recalling his cricketing days in Hollywood in the 1930s he said: 'They must seem very silly nowadays, but they had a touch of the old, home country about them. C. Aubrey Smith was the guiding spirit: he had actually been a cricketer in Britain. Tea, cucumber sandwiches, flannels and our own club blazer . . . David Niven? Didn't see much of him. Turned up a couple of times for our Sunday afternoon sessions. Good spin-bowler, if I remember.'

David Niven remembered it himself with a good deal of personal affection; but he had other games to play. Goldwyn's publicists were building him up as a new Britisher in the style of Ronald Colman and he was aware that there was a great deal to do before he could safely say he had 'arrived', and, of course, there was a lot of fun to be had, much of it with 'the ladies'.

Above left: Nigel Bruce, C. Aubrey Smith and Sir Cedric Hardwicke seem nonplussed by their radio script. Hardwicke was one of the principal organizers of the British movie colony's wartime effort, producing a film for which British stars and directors gave their services free. It was released in 1943, the year in which Hardwicke scored success in a leading role, as the Nazi commander in The Moon is Down *(1943).*

Above right: A dapper, grown-up Freddie Bartholomew, Reginald Gardiner and Madeleine Carroll join David Niven in a charity broadcast. Gardiner specialized in 'silly ass' roles, notably in The Man Who Came to Dinner *(1941) and* Molly and Me *(1945), one of Gracie Fields' American films.*

Making Friends

It was said of Niven that he worked hardest at playing hard. Certainly this was the impression he gave, but his intense socializing was also good policy. He needed to know everybody and the Goldwyn contract was the key to a door he now pushed wide open. He had charm, status and an English accent. In a very short time Niven, while not ditching his English friends, had a host of new American ones.

Niven saw no reason why he should remain in the ghetto of stiff upper lips, so he played tennis with established stars such as Constance Bennett and Gilbert Roland, with Dolores del Rio and art designer Cedric Gibbons, who had decorated many an expensive musical and had designed the Oscar statuette. There was also golf to be played with Jean Harlow and William Powell. 'Golf, though,' he once said,

David Niven at a birthday party for Constance Bennett held at the Trocadero with Dolores del Rio, one of the most beautiful women ever to grace a cinema screen, and her husband Cedric Gibbons, art director at MGM.

'I never really got the hang of. It's a strange game – all your energies are directed inwards towards a small hole, as it were, not outwards as in other games. I suppose it's a lot like sex.'

To keep his social life afloat, however, Niven realized that he needed the raft of steady work. He was, therefore, heeding what Sam Goldwyn had told him, and making himself available for any part, however small. His very first speaking role was at Paramount in 1935 in *Without Regret*. He said 'Goodbye, my dear' to actress Elissa Landi on a railway station platform. An emotional drama, *Without Regret* was co-written by Charles Brackett, who went on to make some remarkable Hollywood films, such as *Sunset Boulevard* (1950), with director Billy Wilder.

His next film was *Barbary Coast* (1935), directed by Howard Hawks, in which he made an impact that only he appreciated. He played a

Opposite: William Powell with his dog Schnapps. MGM provided him with a more celebrated canine companion, Asta, in The Thin Man *(1934), the first of a delightful comedy-thriller series developed from Dashiell Hammett's novel. Powell played the suave, Martini-loving amateur sleuth Nick Charles.*
Above: Gilbert Roland, a Latin lover of the late 1920s who progressed to ruggedly handsome character roles in the 1940s and 1950s.

Left and below: Jean Harlow, the blonde bombshell of the early 1930s, whose uninhibited, wisecracking brand of slatternly trollops still seem fresh and immensely sexy today. Marie Dressler provided her with the perfect epitaph in Dinner at Eight *(1933). Harlow's predatory moll wonders if machinery will replace every profession, to which Dressler tartly replies, 'Oh, my dear, that is something you need never worry about.' It all proved too much for her husband, MGM executive Paul Bern, who committed suicide two weeks after their marriage amid rumours of impotence.*
Opposite: Displaying her car number plate, full of lucky 7s. Ironically, she died in 1937.

cockney sailor who says 'Orl right – I'll go', and is promptly thrown out of a San Franciscan brothel through the window and into the mud.

A Feather in Her Hat (1935) followed: a sob story about literary life and love, it gave Niven his biggest scene so far, as Leo Cartwright, a poet. Niven has himself related how the director, Alfred Santell, got him through the scene on only the second take. He asked the studio crew to applaud Niven however badly he did on the first take, so that with his confidence boosted Niven practically shrugged his way through the scene the second time around.

His first film for Goldwyn himself in which he had a title part was *Splendor* (1935), directed by Elliott Nugent, a riches-to-rags story in which Niven played Clancey Lorrimore, the ne'er-do-well grandson of an upper class family who tries to blackmail his sister-in-law (Miriam Hopkins). Turgid stuff, and it was no wonder that Niven remembered little enough about it in later years. *Palm Springs* and

Opposite: Maurice Chevalier, Marlene Dietrich and Gary Cooper at the première of The Sign of The Cross *(1932). Dietrich had worn a tuxedo in* The Blue Angel *and* Morocco *(both 1930) and her taste for men's clothing sparked off a craze for men's suits.*

Above: Mexican star Lupe Velez cuddles up to boyfriend Gary Cooper after returning from a trip home in 1929. She later married Johnny Weissmuller.

Rose Marie (1936), directed by W. S. Van Dyke – this last a star vehicle for the robust vocal talents of Jeanette MacDonald and Nelson Eddy – followed without leaving a ripple on the pond.

Thank You, Jeeves (1936), directed by Arthur Greville Collins, was more significant. Niven played P. G. Wodehouse's wonderful silly ass character Bertie Wooster, at the mercy of an omnipotent Jeeves, played by Arthur Treacher. Niven has told how he was getting together a 'whole repertory of looks that passed for acting from boggling my eyes to furrowing my brow'. He did himself an injustice. He had a natural gift for comedy acting and he quickly acquired a knack which had been taught him by Charles Chaplin and which could be summed up as: 'Learn to listen to the other actors.'

Niven found some small scope for that in *Bluebeard's Eighth Wife* (1938), in which Niven played the secretary to Gary Cooper's Mr Brandon. Claudette Colbert was Brandon's girlfriend. The film was directed by Ernst Lubitsch, whom he had already met at one of Elsa Maxwell's parties, a wonderful experience for Niven, and one to contrast with his next film for Goldwyn, *Dodsworth* (1936).

This was a reverent adaptation of a Sinclair Lewis novel and starred Walter Huston. It was also directed by William Wyler, who had a reputation for being autocratic to the point of tyranny once behind a camera. Laurence Olivier once told me 'he was one of the most formidable experiences I have ever encountered in film making'.

David Niven said that Wyler reduced him to 'a gibbering wreck'. He recorded that he kept one review of the film which was from the *Detroit Free Press*: 'In this picture we were privileged to see the great Sam Goldwyn's discovery – all we can say about this actor (?) is that he is tall, dark and not the slightest bit handsome.'

In that same year of 1936, though, came a film which was more to Niven's liking, and Hollywood's: *The Charge of the Light Brigade*. Niven, on loan from Goldwyn, met two people on this film who, in their own ways, were to make a great difference to him: the director Michael Curtiz and Errol Flynn. Michael Curtiz was Hungarian and much given to conversing through a loud hailer. An early exponent of 'expressionist' lighting and 'moody' atmosphere, he became one of the smoothest professionals in the business. However, his mangled English and inspired colloquialisms were of an extravagance to match Sam Goldwyn's.

The title of one of Niven's books, in fact, came from Curtiz. During the making of *The Charge of the Light Brigade*, he asked that riderless horses be brought on to the set or as he put it: 'Bring on the empty horses!'

Niven feels he got into the film because he stood up to Curtiz's bullying during audition and that Curtiz ever after did all he could to help him, even building up his role, in *The Charge of the Light Brigade*, of a young British officer on the northwest frontier of India.

There was certainly a ruthless streak to Curtiz, who would drive actors just as hard as his horses. For the animals, his demands could be lethal. Three horses died doing stunts during *The Charge of the Light Brigade* and the production company, Warner Brothers, were fined. Controls over the use of animals were thereafter tightened up.

To Niven though, Michael Curtiz was a subject for giggles not groans. Curtiz spotted him at the side of the set chuckling with a friend at something that Curtiz had just said. He shouted over at them through his loud-hailer: 'You think I know f—— nothing, well, let me tell you – I know f—— all!'

Michael Curtiz may have been especially disconcerted because the friend with whom Niven was laughing, and the star of the film, was Errol Flynn.

Curtiz and Flynn enjoyed sparring or rather Flynn enjoyed anything that made life more interesting. He was a star who, in many

'Bring on the empty horses!' Errol Flynn, director Michael Curtiz and David Niven during the filming of The Charge of the Light Brigade *(1936), a thunderous actioner which bore no relation to historical fact.*

Opposite: On board his yacht the Zacca, Errol Flynn supervises the filming of some marine life, by no means the only form of life which accompanied him on his voyages.
Left: Being made up for his part in The Sea Hawk (1940).
Below left: Despite the image of the lithe swashbuckler, Flynn was an insecure and confused man. Warners handled his peak years with great care, entrusting nineteen of the thirty-one movies he made between 1935 and 1948 to the supremely professional hands of Michael Curtiz and Raoul Walsh.
Below right: For once on his best behaviour dancing with Mrs Jack Warner at Carrolls Restaurant.

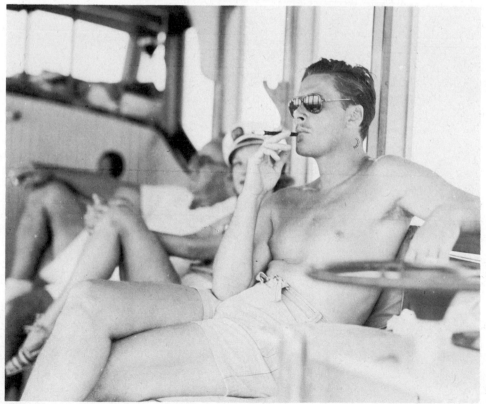

ways, epitomized Hollywood for the general public in the 1930s. His roles were mainly straightforwardly heroic and action packed. He was capable of real acting, but, for the most part, he was never required to do anything in the least bit subtle. His private life, particularly his love life, was just as action packed and just as watchable as his performance on screen, at least so thought thousands of filmgoers. Born in Australia, Flynn described himself as a Tasmanian Devil and after an eventful early life 'roughing it' he came to Hollywood, his perfect habitat – part frontier town, part boom town.

Girls were his principal concern, for he had seemingly set out to prove that no man could ever be bored while there was yet one woman still to be conquered. But drink, and then drugs, helped destroy his career and, later, his life. In his absolute ruthlessness, Flynn was unlike Niven, but he shared Niven's 'stage fright'. He would sometimes throw up before a scene, so scared was he of the outcome. Behind the self-confidence and nonchalance there lurked a nervous man.

Towards the end of his life he became embittered, feeling that the world only regarded him as an enormous phallus. It was an image however, that he had done his best to create.

Flynn was, on my school analogy, the Cad of the Fifth, who raked his way through women captivated by his good looks and easy charm. It is rather touching that, despite Flynn's exalted status, Niven regarded him with almost elder-brother affection, an affection Flynn returned. You could never rely on Errol to do anything except let you down, but Niven, whose recklessness was restrained by basic instincts of self-preservation, was attracted by a man who was untameable, possessed of a courage in the last analysis born of despair.

In his own book *My Wicked Wicked Ways*, it is interesting to note Flynn hardly refers to Niven at all: his was completely self-centred. Niven remained sane because he was always ready to admit the reality of other people – Niven's own autobiographies are about his friends and enemies as much as about himself and Flynn has a starring role.

It was the tradition for unattached male stars to set up in a house or bungalow together. It did not mean that homosexuality was more common in Hollywood than anywhere else; it simply meant that expenses could be shared. The most expensive 'expense' was, of course, women.

Flynn and Niven rented 601, North Linden Drive, Beverly Hills, from actress Rosalind Russell, who, being a devout Catholic, had no illusions about sin and sinners. She promptly baptized the place 'Cirrhosis by the Sea'.

Number 601 became a centre for many amorous intrigues but Niven was to admit that, as far as women were concerned, Flynn led and he followed. Very early on in their residence, Niven recalls that he came home to find the producer Walter Wanger lurking about

worried that his beloved actress Joan Bennett was in danger of assault. Niven was able to assure him that she was not waiting for Flynn in the bed upstairs. Wanger left. Niven was carrying on another school tradition: thou shalt not sneak. Miss Bennett was actually waiting for Flynn in the living-room. . . .

If Niven admired Flynn's derring-do, Flynn himself admired the flamboyance of the great actor John Barrymore, whose talent had become corroded by drink. There is a story, recounted by both Flynn and Niven, and later fictionally re-created in the film *S.O.B.* (1981), that when Barrymore died, Flynn went out drinking to drown his grief. Returning home, much the worse for wear, he found Barrymore sitting in his customary chair, with a drink in his hand. On closer inspection Flynn discovered his friend had not, in fact, risen from the dead. Barrymore's corpse was on loan from a bribed undertaker.

This picture must have been staged as W. C. Fields and John Barrymore, two of Hollywood's most notorious drinkers, have only cups of coffee in front of them. Perhaps this accounts for Fields' agitated expression. It was said that when Fields travelled, he needed three trunks: one for clothes and two for liquor.

71

Flynn was not particularly offended. It was the kind of joke that was wild enough to suit his high-flying temperament. 'Corpse de balls-up!' he would say, having a distinct macho antipathy towards any male dancer with a *corps de ballet*.

There was one joke in which both Flynn and Niven were involved which rebounded, though more on Niven than on the Tasmanian Devil. While at sea yachting, they gave a tow back to Harry Cohn, head of Columbia studios. Back on shore they sent a jokey letter to him claiming salvage. The irate Cohn barred Niven from Columbia for life. Not even an appearance in his office from a contrite Niven lifted the ban, which remained until Cohn died twenty years later.

Cohn was the archetypal school bully of Hollywood. His language was foul, his sexual aggrandizement legendary. He was called 'White Fang' by the screen writer Ben Hecht, and once declared 'I don't have ulcers: I give them.'

It has been said that Cohn had sound stages wired so that he could listen to private conversation, and as a Christmas gift, he promised to fire anyone a favoured secretary pointed at. He also found pleasure in literally giving his guests shocks: one of the chairs in his executive dining-room was wired for electricity. An abominable, formidable

Merle Oberon, with whom David Niven appears in these three pictures, was a delectable woman who owed much to her husband, Alexander Korda. Korda made her a star, as Anne Boleyn, in The Private Life of Henry VIII *(1933) and two years later Goldwyn acquired a share of her contract. She was disastrously miscast as a simpering Cathy in* Wuthering Heights *(1939), but managed to top this performance with a bizarre portrayal of Georges Sand in* A Song to Remember *(1944). Below left: On the set of* Beloved Enemy *(1936), a drama set in the Irish 'Troubles' of 1921, and right: Posing with Niven during the filming of* Raffles *(1939).*

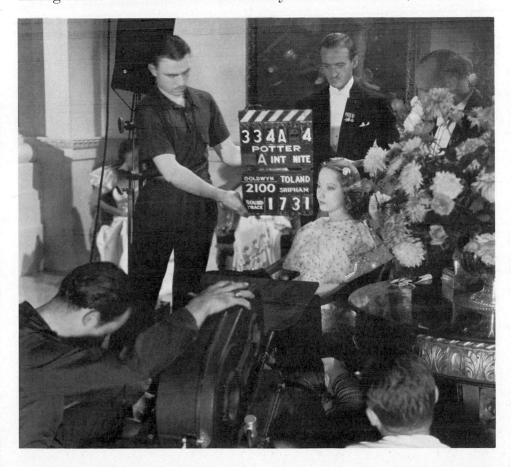

man, yet he made Columbia successful where kinder men might have failed. It was thought there was a certain ruthless self-confidence and native shrewdness which overcame his brutish Nero-like whims so that he would make the right decisions at critical moments. Like Mussolini, he could, as it were, make the trains run on time, though the cost in human terms was great.

All tycoons have their share of megalomania. There is the famous story of Sam Goldwyn, whose publicity executive put a poster on his desk extolling *We Live Again* (1934). It read: 'The directorial genius of Mamoulian, the beauty of Sten and the producing genius of Goldwyn have been combined to make the world's greatest entertainment.' Goldwyn said, 'That's the kind of ad I like. Facts, no exaggeration.' Niven kept everything in perspective because he could always remind himself: 'It is only a film.'

Niven has called Goldwyn 'a father figure' but if he was that, he was also a headmaster figure. Goldwyn assumed that his contract with the actor allowed him to treat Niven virtually as a slave. This was something that Niven did not accept, constantly asserting himself by petty acts of rebellion. Once, when he went on an amorous holiday with a female star, he was pursued all over the country by Goldwyn cablegrams threatening him with dismissal.

There was also the long period during which Niven could not make up his mind whether or not to take the role of Edgar in Goldwyn's next film, *Wuthering Heights* (1939), with Laurence Olivier and Merle Oberon. Eventually, Goldwyn was reduced to pleading with Niven: 'What is it you don't like about the part? I'll go down on my elbows to you . . .' Goldwyn used language like a child uses paints, imprecisely but with colour.

Niven, in fact, liked the role all right. It was the thought of working again with William Wyler that made him hesitate. *Dodsworth* had been a more painful experience than he had admitted at the time.

Eventually, Wyler took him for dinner and promised to be more controlled in his behaviour. Niven agreed to the role of Edgar, only to find that Wyler was just as obstreperous as ever. The school bully could not change his methods, but Niven had to admit that the results which Wyler got were the ones he wanted: good ones.

If Wyler were the bully and Goldwyn the headmaster, Marlene Dietrich might well be termed the school matron, of the most glamorous kind. Niven recalls how once, when he had a bad dose of flu and could not get out of bed, she arrived with soup and medicine. Not only that, she stopped to clean the place up. 'And it wasn't as if I knew her at all well. But I did know her chauffeur and he must have told her. So the door opened and in-flu Marlene.'

She was to become one of Niven's dearest friends. 'She always seemed so very different to me in real life from the siren we saw on the screen. She was, in many ways, very much a Hausfrau.'

Marlene Dietrich dressed as Leda and the Swan at a costume party thrown by Basil Rathbone and his wife. Every feather on her costume was dyed the exact shade of blue to match her eyes. She is accompanied by Countess Dorothy di Frasso, who for a time was Gary Cooper's lover.

Her early mentor was Josef von Sternberg, the distinguished director who was born in Vienna as Josef Stern and emigrated to America, where he altered his name to make it sound more aristocratic. Sternberg's long association with Dietrich produced many fine films, including *The Blue Angel* (1930), *Morocco* (1930), *Shanghai Express* (1932), *The Scarlet Empress* (1934) and *The Devil Is a Woman* (1935).

Their sweet-sour relationship was one of the great Hollywood partnerships. Because of his closeness to her, Sternberg was able to make the connection between the sinuous siren on screen and what he called 'the modest little German Hausfrau' off it: 'She had fashioned a woman who had no existence except on the screen.'

Niven once said: 'Most actors can leave off a role with their make-up. But Hollywood forces you to feel that you're always the role you

Dietrich with her husband Rudolph Sieber and her daughter Maria, who joined her in Hollywood in 1931. In The Scarlet Empress *(1934),* Maria *played the Empress Catherine as a child.*

play. That's typecasting.' Dietrich was at heart a Hausfrau, but she *could* be intimidating. In her long association with von Sternberg, she acquired some of his ruthless need for perfection. Alfred Hitchcock said of her after *Stage Fright* (1950): 'Miss Dietrich is a *professional* – a professional actress, a professional dress designer, a professional camera man!'

This was said with a certain seasoning of acid, but others felt something like awe in the presence of a woman who was so determined to get what she wanted that there were times she would demand, and get, a mirror placed next to the camera lens so that she could look into it and check her lighting.

All an actor or actress had to sell was themselves. Marlene Dietrich wanted to be as flatteringly packaged as possible. Cameraman Lee Garmes said of her: 'She had a great mechanical mind and knew the camera. She would always stop in the exact position that was right for her.'

Charles Laughton, Dietrich, Tyrone Power and director Billy Wilder photographed during the filming of Witness for the Prosecution *(1957).*

Dietrich with her mentor Josef von Sternberg, with whom she made seven classic films: The Blue Angel *(1930)*, Morocco *(1930)*, Dishonored *(1931)*, Shanghai Express *(1932)*, Blonde Venus *(1932)*, The Scarlet Empress *(1934) and* The Devil Is a Woman *(1935)*. *After their split in 1935, neither of them was ever the same again. Below: Visiting Madeleine Carroll on the set, with Clifton Webb and Clark Gable.*

David Niven never gave the impression of taking himself as seriously as all that – 'you must remember that I had no real firm grounding as an actor; I was always grateful that I could get through a scene at all; I suppose my real ability came later.'

Others also burned with the desire for perfection while Niven seemed to fiddle his leisure time away in parties or liaisons with ladies who would kiss and never tell. Cary Grant was one of those whose zeal for self-improvement almost awed Niven.

Alfred Hitchcock standing at a characteristically enigmatic distance from his wife and daughter. He came to Hollywood in 1940 to make Rebecca.

Although born in Bristol, England, and thus belonging to Hollywood's British colony, Grant did not really consider himself one of them. He was a loner, seeking identity through many marriages; a man much more complex than his spruce, alert screen persona would seem to indicate.

Grant's success in Hollywood was not reached without some pain and struggle. He once said: 'If I give the impression of being a man without a problem in the world it is because people with problems always try to give that impression. We are all the opposite of what we appear to be.'

In the search for that success, he had changed his name from Archibald Leach. But that other identity, the child of poor parents forced to earn a living as a music-hall acrobat, was not forgotten. He said: 'I have spent the greatest part of my life fluctuating between Archie Leach and Cary Grant; unsure of either, suspecting each.'

Nobody was allowed to suspect whatever turmoil was going on within that easy-seeming personality. Niven has reported on Grant's fascination with diets; 'today we'll have nothing but carrot juice', and experiments with the drug LSD. His experiments with women were similarly part of a search for new experience and for perfection.

Actors and actresses all longed to be loved, as Cary Grant once remarked. They also wanted tangible evidence of that love in the way of houses, swimming pools and cars. Even their problems were peculiar to success. If you had to have psychological problems, at least you wanted to suffer in comfort.

'I soon realized', said Niven, 'that although it never mattered to me what materialistic success I had attained, it mattered very much in terms of the way other people regarded you.'

Automobiles were symbols for stars as well as for business executives indicating 'fame'. When Niven signed his contract with Goldwyn, his first action was to buy a new Ford. It was not what was called a 'star car' but it would serve for the time being.

Tom Mix, the cowboy star, had a vast vehicle with its motorway-long head adorned with a saddle and steer horns. Clara Bow drove a red Kissel convertible painted to match her hair. Clark Gable had a lengthy customized Duesenberg, which he ordered had to be a foot longer than Gary Cooper's green and yellow one.

To an extent, these can be seen as the playthings given to small children to keep them quiet, but they were also important reflections of personal fantasy. Actors were, for the most part, well aware of their fragile hold on success. They were dispensable. The producers and the moneymen, on the other hand, were secure in their own conviction that *they* were the real powers of Hollywood. Harry Cohn once said: 'Great parts make great pictures! Great pictures make great parts. Kim Novak has had five hit pictures. If you want to bring me your wife or your aunt, we'll do the same for them.'

Class Struggle

'The Americans', Niven once said, 'insist that they have no such thing as class distinction, that they are proud to be a Republic in which everyone has the opportunity to become President. Providing, they forget to add, you have as much money as the Kennedy family.'

On the occasions I met David Niven, politics as such were always relegated to the background of conversation, on the principle that there were two things an English drinking man did not discuss: politics and religion (so I never found out if he was at all religious, although he did say he went through the usual bout of intense faith when he was adolescent).

His comment about the Kennedys is, of course, a truth all visitors to the United States bear witness to. It has a class structure largely based on money and in many ways it is more rigid than the British version. Just at this stage of his career, David Niven was made more aware of it than ever, for he was starting to be taken up by the 'aristocrats' of Hollywood. The great and successful in Hollywood buttressed their status as aristocratic families always have done. They appointed their sons and daughters to important positions and surrounded themselves with lesser mortals to bow and scrape when so required and say 'yes' when asked their advice.

It was not so much the stars who created royal courts for themselves but the studio bosses, who hoped, in their heart of hearts, that their sons or sons-in-law would inherit their empires and that their sons would inherit from them. So must Mussolini have dreamed.

Marrying the boss's daughter has always been good advice to the ambitious, and in Hollywood it was often said that 'the son-in-law also rises'.

Niven found his place in the social whirl, and proved an adept courtier. He was never a 'yes' man, but he did know how to behave and how to be liked.

Cinema audiences in the 1930s were no different from followers of today's 'soap operas'. They did not really expect actors to act. Once a certain role had been established it was best to repeat it in film after film. It would have been an unpleasant and no doubt an unacceptable shock to filmgoers had Errol Flynn appeared in the part of, say, an unsuccessful clerk. Flynn was a hero fighting the same fights in whichever movie he appeared.

I suppose that the first sign that the movies had taken a hold on the public imagination must have come when the mental patient assured his consultant that, no, he was not Jesus Christ or Napoleon, but

Douglas Fairbanks and Mary Pickford, the uncrowned king and queen of Hollywood in the 1920s. Pickford is wearing one of the 'Little Mary' outfits which fixed her screen image in a state of permanently arrested adolescence. Although she did not appear as a little girl until her twenty-fourth feature and constantly tried to vary her roles, it was as Pollyanna (1919) and Little Annie Rooney (1925) that she was cherished by her fans. When she was well into her thirties, she was still dressing up as 'the girl with the golden curls' to welcome important visitors to the studio.

Charlie Chaplin or Douglas Fairbanks Sr. In short, the film stars became for many filmgoers 'friends', alter egos, dreamlike kings and queens to worship and emulate.

For many people in Britain today, the Royal Family occupies that fairy tale position. In the Hollywood of the 1930s, stars such as Gable and his wife Carole Lombard, Garbo or Dietrich satisfied the same need. The important thing for the film producers to remember, and they seldom forgot it, was that the real world was rarely required. There was plenty of poverty, dirt and despair without putting it up on the silver screen.

It was not just private scandals that had to be hushed up, it was necessary to preserve a star's image on screen. A deviation from the role that the public had become used to could be not merely difficult for audiences to accept but positively damaging. One small-town American cinema manager complained to the film's distributors: 'To me *Sing You Sinners* was ruined by about 200 feet of film showing

Doug and Mary take a little canoe trip at their magnificent Hollywood home known to one and all as Pickfair. In the 1920s it became a Californian version of the White House and an important port of call for visiting notables. Dickie Mountbatten made home movies on the lawn; the Queen of Siam graced the tennis courts; and on one memorable occasion, Albert Einstein used a fork and dinner plate to demonstrate the theory of relativity to the bemused guests.

Above left: Mary Pickford and her film crew. Seated next to her with his arms folded is Charles Rosher, a brilliant cameraman and technical innovator, and the masterly photographer of Mary's golden ringlets, which he used to arrange himself on the set. In the 1920s, he was the highest paid cameraman in the world.
Above right: Mary Pickford with Gary Cooper and Marion Davies and left: relaxing at Pickfair. After her divorce from Fairbanks, she married actor Charles 'Buddy' Rogers. In the 1960s, Pickford became a bed-ridden recluse and Pickfair a mausoleum. There was an ever present bottle of whisky at her side and, at her insistence, all the distressing items were cut out from the daily newspapers before these were given to her.

Bing Crosby intoxicated. I don't know how you feel about scenes dealing with the stars getting intoxicated, but I do know that about 75 per cent lose a lot of interest in any star who has had the misfortune to be so cast . . . let the supporting cast do the drinking.' Eighty-five million picturegoers in America and more than twenty million in Britain could not be contradicted.

Yet the real world would keep on making itself felt. After all, Hollywood was a town inhabited by hundreds of people living artificial lives under impossible pressures and plagued by feelings of insecurity. To begin with there was the drinking. Alcohol assuaged insecurity better than almost anything; most stars felt they were involved in a confidence trick and that at any moment somebody would come along and announce that the game was up and all the loot had to be given back. It is hard to relax when you are afraid.

'One way for the top people to prove their superiority over the others', said Niven 'was to give parties – wild, extravagant parties,

Hedda Hopper (above left) and Louella Parsons seen here (above right) in 1935 with Dick Powell and Jean Harlow. Hedda and Louella were gossip column arch rivals who in their heyday shared a combined readership of about 75 million. Hopper was a failed actress who in the 1920s had been dubbed 'Queen of the Quickies' by a considerate Louella Parsons. Hedda's son William enjoyed brief fame as Perry Mason's private eye Paul Drake in the long-running television series.

each one being better than the one before. And there were always Louella and Hedda to write about them next day. Without them could one be sure the party had been a success or, worse still, that you ever existed?'

Louella Parsons and Hedda Hopper were the two top gossip columnists, who felt that around them the whole of Hollywood, if not the whole universe, revolved. Even they, however, were in awe of the newspaper tycoon William Randolph Hearst.

David Niven has written: 'Mr Hearst fascinated me.' It is an unconscious acknowledgement of the awesome strength of the man that Niven called him 'Mr'. Here was not just a headmaster figure but a man whom headmasters called headmaster.

Niven had met him and his film-star mistress, the blonde Marion Davies, on the tennis courts. The friendship was to be further cemented as Niven embarked on a new movie, *The Prisoner of Zenda* (1937), which was to mark another stage of his career. 'Their own mansion

Former Ziegfeld show girl Marion Davies with (above left) her patron and lover, newspaper baron William Randolph Hearst, who spent over $7 million in his bid to turn her into the 'first lady of the screen'. Hearst instructed each one of his papers to mention Marion at least once every day, but not even the effusions of Louella Parsons could endear her to the public. Davies was an actress whose talent was limited, but she had a light comic touch, as she showed in King Vidor's Show People *(1928).*

looked so much like the Ruritanian castle in the movie it was ridiculous.'

William Randolph Hearst was a billionaire newspaper magnate on whom Orson Welles based the megalomaniac tycoon of *Citizen Kane* (1941). Though writer-director Billy Wilder has remarked with some wit: 'Hearst objected to the way he was turned into Kane. He should have been grateful – Kane had character.'

Certainly, Hearst was supposed to be a colourless man, but with money and power on such a scale, probably character was a luxury he could forgo. Undoubtedly, the love of his life was Marion Davies.

Like Kane's Susan Alexander, Marion Davies enjoyed struggling with huge jigsaw puzzles at Hearst's vast residence, San Simeon. But unlike Susan, she was a subtle comedy actress of some wit and

Opposite and above: San Simeon, the ocean-side palace built by William Randolph Hearst which formed the model for Xanadu in Orson Welles' Citizen Kane *standing in a vast estate, it had its own private zoo and, according to the housekeeper, cost $7000 a day to maintain. In* Bring on the Empty Horses *David Niven recalled that on one visit he slept in a bed which had at one time belonged to Cardinal Richelieu.*

intelligence. She met Hearst while she was with the Ziegfeld Follies and remained with him until his death in 1950.

In fact, Hearst founded Cosmopolitan Films to display her talent and Niven met the two of them via Sam Goldwyn, with whom Cosmopolitan was negotiating. Hearst was the ultimate sugar daddy, but to be fair to Marion Davies, she was not just along for the money, she found something to love within his ungainly frame.

Niven once told me that he was convinced that Hearst was angry about *Citizen Kane* not so much because of the portrayal of himself, after all, it was rather flattering in some respects, but because he felt the Susan Alexander character was a slander on Marion. 'Marion was never as empty-headed as that, she had some refinement,' he

Hearst's tormentor Orson Welles with Lucille Ball. After the release of Citizen Kane, *his name disappeared from the Hearst newspapers. Although it is superficially a portrait of Hearst, the passage of time and the blighting of Welles' career have given* Citizen Kane *a strongly autobiographical flavour.*

said. The director King Vidor who directed Marion Davies in three movies, considered her 'a most accomplished comedienne'.

Niven has described parties at San Simeon among those avidly collected antiquities for which Hearst (and Kane) was famous. He remembered hearing the jungle sounds of animals in the night from Hearst's private zoo. 'It sounded like Hollywood tycoons fighting – or mating.'

Vidor was similarly impressed. The estate stretched over two hundred thousand acres and the splendour was reminiscent of Louis XIV's Versailles.

Left to right: Marion Davies, William Haines, King Vidor, Ulric Bush and Eileen Perry during the filming of Show People *(1928). This photograph was taken on the old Mack Sennett lot shortly before it was pulled down.*

Constance Bennett with (left) her second husband, the Marquis de la Falaise de Coudraye, and (below) her daughter Lilybet during a break from filming Born to Love *(1951) with Joel McCrea. Her films are seldom revived today, but in the early 1930s she was one of the highest paid female stars in Hollywood and the queen of the sob-strewn confession movie. In 1931 her agent Myron Selznick secured $30,000 a week for Warners to make* Bought, *a record at the time. An accomplished actress, she later moved smoothly into comedy, starring in such classics as* Topper *(1937) and* Merrily We Live *(1938).*

Above left: Constance's equally famous sister Joan who, at sixteen, ran away with a millionaire and had a child. She had made some forty films before she changed from blonde to brunette in Trade Winds *(1938). This lifted her career at a time when that of her blonde sister Constance (above right) was about to enter decline.*
Left: Joan Bennett at her wedding in 1932 to screen writer Gene Markey. She later married Walter Wanger, the producer who masterminded her career.

Vidor described Hearst as having a 'big lamb-like face', but it could turn stern if he thought that Marion Davies was being affronted – if, for instance, a guest was so injudicious as to mock her stutter. *She* did not mind, but the sugar daddy could turn very sour. Similarly, he objected when Vidor wanted Marion to be smashed in the face with a custard pie for a film about Hollywood. Vidor himself stood in for her, to show how effective it would be. Hearst would have none of it. His mistress must be treated with dignity even in a farce.

'King's right. But I'm right too – because I'm not going to let Marion be hit in the face with a pie,' he insisted and the custard pie, after much wrangling, was exchanged for soda from a siphon.

Plenty of soda and even more alcohol were being splashed into drinks at San Simeon parties. One of the frequent partygoers there was Constance Bennett, a pert, funny actress who became a good friend of Niven's.

Her image has strangely faded in the public mind, but she was one of the highest-paid actresses in Hollywood in the 1930s. Her younger sister, Joan Bennett, was equally successful. Constance's temperament was legendary. When she was going to make a film called *Outcast Lady* (1934) she demanded the services of Charles Rosher as cameraman. He was specially skilled at soft focus photography that was kind to ageing skins. But Rosher was already working with Helen Hayes on *What Every Woman Knows* (1934). So strong was Constance Bennett's influence that he was pulled off the Helen Hayes film halfway through production. Constance Bennett is reported to have said: 'The old focus is more at home on me than on Helen.'

She behaved with all the hauteur of an aristocrat, always giving the impression that she was in Hollywood and yet not of it. Her air of amused contempt was vastly helped by her marriage to the Marquis de la Falaise. All the world loves a lover, but Hollywood specially adored an aristocratic one. Marion Davies had a fourteen-room luxury bungalow in the grounds of MGM, and Constance Bennett's apartments were nearly as luxurious. According to Niven, 'It was almost possible to get lost within them.' She was an expert and devoted poker player, owned a cosmetic company and was a formidable negotiator for her own salary. Niven had first met her in his early days as an extra, when his accent had given him the entrée to the famous.

In *Bring on the Empty Horses*, Niven wrote a profile of her based on a radio broadcast they made together, rehearsals for which were constantly put off by her. To him 'she seemed . . . the quintessence of a Movie Queen. She radiated glamour from her exalted position in the Hollywood firmament and everything about her shone. . . .'

Her chauffeur used to sit outside her black Rolls-Royce Phaeton while she sat behind in the lined compartment, a queen in velvet. One cannot imagine her ever doing a Dietrich and cleaning up after Niven in the sick room.

David O. Selznick. The O. was added later in life and, according to Selznick, stood for Oliver. Selznick was a mogul with real flair; at MGM in 1935 he chose W. C. Fields to play Micawber in David Copperfield, *one of the inspired strokes of casting in film history. As an independent, it took him three years to prepare and shoot* Gone with the Wind *(1939). The stream of memos which accompanied the epic production reveal his skill as an entrepreneur and his obsession with the tiniest details of the films under his control.*

Niven once likened her to Princess Flavia in *The Prisoner of Zenda*; she possessed a kind of unattainable purity while managing to exude sexuality.

The Prisoner of Zenda is *the* great wish-fulfilling romance: it is the story of how the commoner Rudolph Rassendyll stands in for the debauched prince about to be crowned king, and falls for the betrothed princess, who senses in Rudolph more nobility than in her true intended.

Ronald Colman was both king and commoner and Niven's role was that of Fritz van Tarlenheim, aide-de-camp to the king – a role more of dash and *brio* than of any depth, but one that required much technique. It was made before *Wuthering Heights* (1939), but Niven always regarded it as being central to his development as a film actor.

'The son-in-law also rises'. David O. Selznick with his bride Irene Mayer and his father-in-law Louis B. Mayer at the Biltmore Hotel, August 1930.

It was one of the first times that he felt 'at home' in a role; hitherto, despite appearances to the contrary, he had found himself feeling clumsy and inexpert.

'That old problem of an actor's was mine in spades – what to do with my hands. So I *flaunted* them, I used them an awful lot. In some of my early movies I seem to have them continually stuck out in front of me – just like Boris Karloff in *Frankenstein*.'

As a hunk of hokum, this version of *The Prisoner of Zenda* is still the most effective and it gathered together some of the finest members of the British colony, from C. Aubrey Smith through Colman to Douglas Fairbanks Jr.

Niven had become a firm friend of Colman and Douglas Fairbanks Jr. As a friend of Douglas Fairbanks Jr he also came to know well Fairbanks Sr and Mary Pickford, the nearest to true aristocracy in Hollywood.

Producer David O. Selznick, who was making *The Prisoner of Zenda* was fascinated by Hollywood's past, of which he considered Fairbanks Sr and Pickford to be living legends. 'They and people like them created it all out of nothing; they built it with their own bare hands and courage.

'We're a different breed these days, but I hope we still have the guts and ability to do what's right to make movies such a force.'

Niven found that Selznick, one of the most irascible and successful of all the independent producers, was a man of captivating charm. He was convinced that Selznick won him (Niven) from Goldwyn for *The Prisoner of Zenda* in a card game. Selznick always treated him with a courtesy Niven greatly appreciated. There was only one cross word between them and that was when Selznick did not think that Niven and Colman were putting in enough fencing practice.

Selznick's admiration for the past possibly originated from his love of his father, Louis, an early partner of Louis B. Mayer, by 1937 the lachrymose and lethal boss of Metro Goldwyn Mayer. Louis Selznick, too, had been one of the pioneers of the industry, but rumour had it that Mayer had ruined his career. Selznick and his brother Myron, the most formidable agent in Hollywood, were said to have sworn to get Mayer. To compound the irritation that Mayer must undoubtedly have felt at having David Oliver Selznick as a rival, the man became his son-in-law!

Selznick never reckoned Mayer himself as one of the founding fathers of Hollywood, but it was rumoured that Selznick had insisted on Douglas Fairbanks Jr playing the role of Rupert of Hentzau in the movie as a tribute to Fairbanks Sr and Mary Pickford.

It seems a strangely innocent motive for a man who was, in every way, a fiendishly astute businessman and, of course, it proved a shrewd piece of casting. Fairbanks Jr's performance stole the film. He portrayed the sinister lieutenant to Black Michael, played by

Mary Astor on the links in her silent days with First National, 1924–28. One of Hollywood's most independent spirits, she was at her best playing demure bitches or double-dealing femmes fatales, including Brigid O'Shaughnessy in The Maltese Falcon *(1941). A divorce action of 1936 produced a sensation when torrid extracts from her diaries were revealed in court.*

Raymond Massey, and he created one of the most delightfully villainous rogues in cinema.

For Niven it was one of the most enjoyable experiences in his Hollywood years. His role was not a major one, but he enjoyed the camaraderie of it all. The women were lovely to look at, Madeleine Carroll was Flavia, and there was even some scurrility to spice the whole affair so that it would not seem too bland.

Mary Astor, who played Madame de Mauban, became the focus of sensation because of her published diaries, which recounted the prowess of her many lovers. . . .

Years later Niven was to talk about *Zenda* days as being some of the happiest of his life. One can see why. Ruritania was a dream of

Joan Crawford and her first husband, Douglas Fairbanks Jr, set sail for Europe aboard the liner 'Bremen' in 1932. They were divorced two years later.

a world that never was, but ought to have existed. It was a vision, in fact, of an England combining Arthurian chivalries with Edwardian codes of manliness.

Ruritania was a land frozen within its own myth and time, rather like Niven's Hollywood. It was a world with which Niven was by now familiar. He knew his way around and could enjoy its intrigues and mad logic. Perhaps it was all hollow, nothing but a cardboard sham, but Niven was to say later of those years that if he had found nothing else he had found friendship. 'And that's an awful lot to get out of life. Luck had a great deal to do with it.'

David Niven pays the bill after a night out at the Trocadero with Madeleine Carroll, one of Britain's most glamorous exports to America, whose cool English rose looks were perfectly suited to fairytale romances like The Prisoner of Zenda *(1937).*

Almost a Star

Niven very quickly became a successful Hollywood actor. The roles he was offered grew more important and interesting. None the less, though he was in line for starring roles, he never quite attained the ultimate status of a star in the way Errol Flynn, Ronald Colman or Clark Gable did. In part this was because he did not care enough. He was not a ruthless, ambitious man and was content with the secure

The Big Four: Mary Pickford, D. W. Griffith, Charles Chaplin and Douglas Fairbanks Sr, founders in 1919 of United Artists.

Charlie Chaplin's Hollywood home. The barbed wire fence gives it a slightly sinister aspect.

and privileged life he had in his own view so magically achieved. In these golden, Goldwyn years before the outbreak of World War II, he enjoyed to the full a charmed existence. Outside, he was only too well aware, there was economic depression, unforgiving cold reality. Who can blame him for preferring tinsel and glitter, however insubstantial?

'Oh yes, we were lucky in those days,' Niven has written, 'and most of us who were there realised it.' Niven had, of course, paid his dues as an 'extra', he was forever afterwards bitter about the 'Meat Market', where aspirants for small roles would be required to audition in humiliating conditions and treated with degrading contempt by producers and directors. At the same time, he did not see himself as a knight in shining armour. There were plenty of causes to espouse, but none that touched him personally.

'The Americans are great signers of petitions and things for the good of everything,' he has said. 'I don't think I signed one petition on behalf of anyone.'

The last years of the 1930s were a time for causes. President Roose- velt was giving public expression to many people's belief in social responsibility. Niven was no more heartless than the next man, but he had been educated in a rough school and did not hastily reveal a bleeding heart. It was part of his image that an English gentleman did not give way to emotions. The upper lip must remain stiff.

Niven was immensely loyal to the people he liked or admired and was, for instance, very angry at the way Charlie Chaplin was treated by Hollywood when the chaos of his sexual life was revealed to envious and spiteful eyes. Chaplin was one of those Niven thought of as 'top of the class' and he knew it was inevitable that lesser men would want to bring him down. Charlie's son, Charlie Junior, has noted: 'My father seemed to have become resigned to the fact that a living artist's work will always be judged more or less through the perspective of his personal life.'

Niven knew two of Chaplin's wives: Mildred Harris Chaplin and Paulette Goddard, by whom he was particularly enchanted. There

Charlie Chaplin and Eric Campbell try an early version of Fred Astaire's famous golf ball routine in The Idle Class *(1922).*

99

Opposite: Chaplin during the filming of Shoulder Arms (1918), the second film he made at First National.

Left: About to set off on a flight to Catalina with Captain Amory Rogers. Many Hollywood stars were keen pilots, including Ruth Chatterton, Ray Milland, Roy Speary and James Stewart.

Below left: Pictured in 1926 with his son Charles Jr and his second wife, Lita Gray.

Below right: His first wife Mildred Harris, an MGM extra whom Chaplin married in 1918. They were divorced in 1921.

Michael Brook, Paulette Goddard and David Niven watch an American Legion boxing match.

was something spritely, almost otherworldly about her which delighted and charmed him. Chaplin's personal and sexual life seems to have been as unruly as his professional life was ordered and contained. His genius was original and unchallengeable, arising perhaps from a childlike, naïve egoism fused with absolute technical mastery. His politics were liberal rather than Communist, but helped to make him suspect in the eyes of powerful men. His enemies found in his sexual peccadilloes a way to persecute him.

Chaplin once defined the difference between comedy and tragedy: 'If you boot a person up the backside just the right amount then that's farce, but if you boot him too hard then that's tragic.'

Chaplin's own life was always veering between tragedy and farce in exactly this way. In common with every other public figure in

Left: Charlie Chaplin and
Paulette Goddard at the famous
Brown Derby restaurant. One of
a long line of gamines taken up
by Chaplin (Edna Purviance was
the first), Goddard starred in
Modern Times (1936) and The
Great Dictator (1940).
Married to Chaplin from 1935 to
1942, she was by far the most
appealing of his leading ladies.
She later married Burgess
Meredith, with whom she appeared
in The Diary of a Chambermaid
(1946), and then the writer
Erich Maria Remarque.
Below: Goddard with H. G.
Wells, whom she met at the
première of The Great Dictator
and, so the story goes, pursued
across America while he gave a
lecture tour.

Hollywood, he was at the mercy of astute and unprincipled gossip columnists, including the two most predatory, Louella Parsons and Hedda Hopper.

Niven has written about both Parsons and Hopper with a kind of amused distaste, but he got on reasonably well with both of them. Indeed, he went to considerable trouble not to cross them.

They were a strange, awesome duo, not unlike Macbeth's witches. Inevitable rivals, they had the power to destroy reputations, careers and marriages and used that power mercilessly. Strangely, it was Marion Davies who was responsible for both of these women reaching such a position in Hollywood.

Louella Parsons was working for Hearst's *American* in New York. Marion Davies invited her to Hollywood and she soon discovered it was the honeypot around which she could buzz and sting most effectively. She hated what she called 'intellectuals', which meant anyone whom she suspected of thinking themselves superior to her. Her husband, Dr Harry Martin, was an alcoholic, a problem Louella accepted with equanimity. She is reported to have said on one occasion when told that he had passed from being jocose to comatose: 'Don't disturb him – he has to operate tomorrow.'

Harry Martin, known to all as 'Dockie', had a $30,000-a-year job as studio physician at Twentieth Century-Fox. It was very much a sinecure; Fox wanted to buffer itself against Miss Parsons's spite and keeping her husband sweet seemed one sure way of doing that.

Left: Louella Parsons shares a
joke with Rosalind Russell.
Rosalind's nervous smile reflects
the fact that dealing with Louella
was rather like handling a
bad-tempered rattlesnake. Few
stars had the courage to snub her,
although Joan Bennett once sent
her a skunk as a Valentine gift.
Below: In her fearless pursuit
of the Big Story, Louella joins
in as Cecil B. De Mille presents
Amos 'n' Andy with an award
recording their ten years
in radio.

Louella Parsons ruled the roost for much of the 1930s, but, in 1935, along came Hedda Hopper, who began writing fashion articles about Hollywood for the *Washington Post*. Again, it was Marion Davies who helped this failed actress become an important source of gossip and rumour. She and Louella Parsons vied with each other as to who was queen bee in the world of Hollywood gossip, but there were others who could not be safely ignored, such as Sheilah Graham, who became F. Scott Fitzgerald's mistress. Almost as bad as being the object of one of these women's vendettas was to be caught by one of them delivering a scoop to the other. A star favouring Louella Parsons with titbits of information would soon find him or herself pilloried by Hedda Hopper and vice versa.

They were not, as one would expect, averse to a little blackmail, but, surprisingly, the majority of stars took it all fairly calmly. In the days before television the gossip columnists, though dangerous enemies, were also valuable image makers. Some stars could not prevent themselves retaliating, however. Joan Bennett sent Hopper a skunk as a present on St Valentine's Day. Merle Oberon once asked why Hopper had been attacking her so virulently lately and got the answer, 'It's bitchery, sheer bitchery.'

It was Merle Oberon, too, who said: 'I feel as though I ought to telephone Hedda or Louella after every love-making, just in case I have conceived. They would want to be the first to know.'

Niven magnanimously wrote: 'They had delusions of grandeur and skins like brontosauruses, but they were gallant, persevering and often soft hearted.'

They helped some beginners, hindered others and interfered in casting, but what could not be doubted was their devotion to Hollywood. They saw their task as one of presenting a dream of Hollywood, preserving in aspic its image as a city of glamour and intrigue, triumph and disaster.

Niven once said: 'How we stood for them I don't know, but we did. Hollywood in those days – much more than it became later – was very much a village. I suppose we just accepted their right to tell us about ourselves.'

One star who seemed to rise above all this was Greta Garbo. Although stories about her appeared regularly in the Press, notably when she was supposed to be having a love affair with the conductor Leopold Stokowski, she managed to retain an air of icy contempt for trivial gossip and intrigue.

One minor gossip columnist, Sidney Skolsky, managed to inveigle his way on to a film set where Garbo was filming, but he was caught and summarily ejected. By keeping aloof and mysterious, she became desirable. The more she tried to avoid the spotlight of public attention, the more it pursued her. Whether deliberately or not, Greta Garbo's queenly disdain for Hollywood made her most prey to gossip

Louella with her husband Dr Harry Martin, whose nickname was 'Dockie'. At the time of their marriage he was house doctor to Hollywood's choicest bordello. A urologist who specialized in venereal disease, his contacts provided Louella with a hot line to Hollywood's most intimate secrets. A hopeless alcoholic, he was provided with a $30,000 a year sinecure as studio physician at Paramount.

and speculation. The aura of silence, the deliciously Swedish accent, 'I want to be alone'. . . . It was quite irresistible.

Niven has recounted how he first saw Garbo during a lunch break when he was working as an extra. She was performing her beloved 'exercises', which, in this case, meant jogging. A Mexican boy pursued her to try to get her autograph but was soon left behind in the dust from her flying feet.

Later Niven got to know her better, but, even after she had accompanied him and another friend on a cramped trip in a small boat, 'normally an infallible way of getting to know someone,' when they docked at San Pedro, he realized he knew her no better than when they had set out.

The legend of Great Garbo, born Greta Gustaffsson, is a powerful one. Niven believed she left Hollywood and films because she had succumbed to vertigo, suddenly realizing how high she had climbed and losing the confidence to climb further.

She told him once: 'I had made enough faces.'

She may have seemed cold, but to her close friends she was warm and loyal. One such friend and lover was the actor John Gilbert, who was destroyed by the coming of the talking pictures. When his film *His Glorious Night* (1929) was premièred at New York's Capitol Theatre, his voice was heard to be light and tinny, almost effeminate. The rumour was that Louis B. Mayer, who wanted to crush the star, had engineers manipulate the sound. Certainly, a later film,

Opposite: Garbo and Gilbert who formed the greatest romantic partnership of the 1920s are reunited in Queen Christina *(1933), Gilbert's last big film. Garbo insisted on him as her leading man. The confidence and vitality of his silent days had drained away and the strain of the comeback is etched into a face ravaged by alcohol. Garbo's gaze is steady and filled with affection. Above left: A virtually unrecognizable Garbo arrives in Hollywood in 1925 with her Svengali, the Swedish director Mauritz Stiller. Louis B. Mayer took one look at Garbo and told Stiller that 'American men don't like fat women'; and right: Garbo with Stiller and (left) their fellow director Victor Seastrom. Seastrom returned to Sweden in 1930 after directing Lillian Gish in* The Wind.

Downstairs (1932), written by Gilbert himself, showed him to have a rather agreeable light tenor. However, the damage had been done; the fans rejected him but Garbo remained loyal, even though they were, by now, no longer lovers. She insisted on his having a role in *Queen Christina* (1933) and helped him financially after he became one of the victims of the Wall Street Crash.

Director Clarence Brown, who worked on many films with Garbo, declared: 'Garbo had something behind the eyes that you couldn't see until you photographed it in close-up. If she had to look at one person with jealousy and another with love she didn't have to change her expression. You could see it in her eyes as she looked from one to another.'

One of her alleged lovers was the great Shakespearian actor, John Barrymore, whom Flynn idolized. David Niven was not, however, as mesmerized. 'I never quite understood Errol's hero worship of John Barrymore. Still of blazing talent and unquestioned, if somewhat blurred profile, he seemed to go out of his way to shock and be coarse: he was also conspicuously unclean and often smelled highly.'

Niven, though, was recalling Barrymore in decline when he could no longer remember his lines and had to read from idiot boards held up for him behind the camera. Nevertheless, even at that terminal stage in his career, Barrymore was capable of being splendidly outrageous. Drink, though, unravelled the fine fabric of his undoubted art. It led him into some dire escapades. Once, inebriated, he wandered into the ladies' lavatory by mistake. A woman followed him.

'This is for women!' she yelled.

'And so, madame, is this', said Barrymore, pointing.

David Niven recalled: 'He lived on a reputation made when he was younger. That was when he and his brother Lionel and sister Ethel made up a royal family on Broadway, although even on stage his drinking was out of control.'

On one occasion, in a period piece, he was supposed to draw a sword and slash Lionel. But the sword broke in its scabbard, so John tried to take out a pistol; no use. Lionel had, by this time, collapsed on the stage with suppressed laughter. Barrymore kicked him and his brother subsided. John strode to the front of the stage and confided to the audience: 'The shoe was poisoned.'

For Barrymore the stage was all; his film work he felt to be of secondary importance and not worthy of his talents. Niven had a very different attitude to making movies. Barrymore, he felt, was lucky to be treated with so much respect when he appeared to make so little effort to be professional. Niven had never been a stage actor, and he knew how hard it had been for him to get where he had and he had no wish to bite the hand that fed him. He was in demand now as a film actor, his career was prospering: 'I never thought of myself as a competitor, but I suppose I was. You had to be.'

John Barrymore and his bride, Dolores Costello. They fell in love while filming The Sea Beast *(1926). Marriage to Barrymore must have been a trial. In the early 1930s, when he was trying to control his alcoholism, he was reduced to drinking the perfume on Costello's dressing-table.*

As silent screen actress Mae Murray once said: 'We were like dragonflies. We seemed to be suspended effortlessly in the air, but in reality our wings were beating very, very fast.'

It is an attractive element in Niven's character that even at his most successful he remained innocently enthusiastic about those whom he considered 'the super, super stars'. He could not seriously see himself as a rival to Flynn or Barrymore, princes in Hollywood. The king was Clark Gable.

John Barrymore, accompanied by his pet monkey Clementina (a present from Gladys Cooper) and the crew of his yacht 'Mariner', a 93-foot gaff-rigged schooner.

'There were Giants in the Earth'

David Niven once wrote, in that self-disparaging way so suited to the English gentleman, that he had been lucky to have stretched 'a minimal talent into a long career'. Thus might Clark Gable have spoken about himself. Gable was referred to as the king, but uneasy lies the head that wears the crown, particularly on ears which producer Irving Thalberg had been so rude about. Gable, however, was undoubtedly one of the natural aristocrats of Hollywood.

Niven met Gable for the first time when he hired a spear fishing boat that Niven was working on in his early days in Hollywood. Later, when Niven got his contract with Goldwyn, Gable made sure that he greeted Niven warmly whenever the two men met, aware that such public recognition could do Niven nothing but good.

Gable's brash, extrovert manner may have been a mask, but Niven did not think so; and anyway, once a mask has been worn long enough it becomes the real face. Gable was a breezy, open man whose roles were usually rough, tough and buccaneering. The archetypal Gable role was, of course, Rhett Butler in *Gone with the Wind* (1939). Frankly, my dear, as he so famously said to Vivien Leigh's Scarlett O'Hara, he did not give a damn, not even about his public image. That was for others to worry about. The rule that he followed, with complete consistency, was what he called 'Spencer Tracy's Formula'. An actor should arrive on time, know the lines and say them the best way possible, take the money and go home at six o'clock.

According to Niven, he said: I'm just out in front of a team, that's all. Metro have half a dozen people, top writers, whose only job is to find the best possible properties for me, things that I fit into with the least risk of falling on my ass . . . that way I remain valuable to them and everyone's happy – for the moment.'

He had known, though, the reverse side of that happy moment, the time of betrayal. Under contract to MGM, he had been loaned out to Harry Cohn's Columbia studios as a kind of punishment for turning down too many poor scripts. It was expected that he would crawl back with his tail between his legs after such an experience with a studio which was certainly not a rich one and where facilities were minimal.

But Gable returned with an Oscar, for the film had been *It Happened One Night* (1934), and Gable was king of the heap again.

He told Niven: 'Don't ever let them kick you around. They squeeze people dry and then drop them . . . when you start to fade they put you into 'skid' pictures so you'll turn them down and they can put

Carole Lombard photographed on the set of The Princess Comes Across *(1936), a delightful comedy thriller co-starring Fred MacMurray and directed by William K. Howard. One of the most captivatingly beautiful and witty actresses of the 1930s, she excelled in screwball comedy. Four of her forty-two films are classics,* Twentieth Century *(1934),* My Man Godfrey *(1936),* Nothing Sacred *(1937) and* To Be Or Not To Be *(1942). She died tragically young, aged thirty-four, in an aircraft crash in 1942.*

Opposite: Clark Gable and Carole Lombard conducted one of Hollywood's most public romances before marrying in 1939. At one point she presented him with a jalopy painted with red hearts. Lombard was a wisecracker whose favourite expression was 'Kiss my ass'. She once appeared on the set of a film in which she thought Gable's co-star was trying to make off with him and booted the lady up the backside. She was just right for Gable, and he never really recovered from her death.
Left: Gable and Joan Crawford with a small friend.
Below left: Gable, Ed Sullivan and Fanny Brice.
Below right: Gable, Lombard and Tyrone Power at the première of Marie Antoinette (1938), *which starred Norma Shearer.*

you on suspension and get you off the payroll . . . be tough with them when you get up there.'

Gable was tough on himself in his leisure time, living the life of a true athlete. He was a huntin', shootin' and fishin' man and found a suitably raucous mate in Carole Lombard, after several marital experiments which fizzled out in very expensive divorce settlements.

Carole Lombard was a woman with an explosively bawdy streak, a cackle of a laugh and an ability to give as good as she got. She made fun of the size of Gable's sexual equipment at parties and he just grinned sheepishly. They had lived together before marriage, a scandalous arrangement in Hollywood in the 1930s. The fan magazine *Photoplay* listed Lombard and Gable, Constance Bennett and Gilbert Roland, Robert Taylor and Barbara Stanwyck, Paulette Goddard and Charles Chaplin as 'Hollywood's Unmarried Husbands and Wives' and this list was by no means supposed to be a roll of honour.

Gable was well aware of the irony of being labelled a great lover. Once he took out his dentures, clacked them at Carole Lombard and said: 'What price the world's greatest lover now?'

Gable was a king who never took himself too seriously, realizing that his throne was as temporary as John Gilbert's had proved to be.

John Gilbert had earned in his heyday $250,000 a film, while in 1931 Gable worked for $350 a week. By 1941 his yearly salary had mounted to $357,500, but, perhaps because of his German-Dutch parentage, he never became a big spender.

Gable was important enough to ensure he got what he wanted. He worked a strict nine-to-five day, and there was even a clause in his contract to say that he would not fly in planes with fewer than two engines. The irony was that Carole Lombard was to die in a plane crash. . . .

This least fashion-conscious of male stars created new fashions in the way pop stars do today. When he was revealed in *It Happened One Night* as wearing no vest or undershirt, to the alarm of the undergarment industry, millions of men suddenly decided it was unmanly to wear anything beneath their shirts. On another occasion, he wore a turtle-neck sweater to match his suits, and the fans imitated him. 'I don't think that's what acting's all about,' he is reported as saying. 'But, as sure as dammit, it's what being a *star* is all about.'

One cannot talk about Clark Gable without mentioning *Gone with the Wind*, that extraordinary epic evocation of the American Civil War. To read it today is still to feel the power of Margaret Mitchell's sub-Tolstoyan account of a family at war. The great American public suddenly realized that they, as well as England and Scotland, had a history. For Hollywood, it was the god-given answer to every mogul's prayer for a film epic.

Below left: John Gilbert, for whom fate reserved one final indignity before he died in 1936 from a heart attack brought on by drink. While dancing in a Hollywood nightclub, the Great Lover's toupee fell off.

Below right: Barbara Stanwyck, never one of the great box-office attractions but one of the truly great stars, a professional to her fingertips. Cecil B. De Mille said of her, 'I have never worked with an actress who was more co-operative, less temperamental and a better workman.'

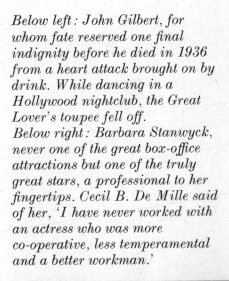

Left: Joan Crawford (left) and Dorothy Sebastian tone up on the beach at Santa Monica.
Below: Crawford gives some publicity stills a careful scrutiny. In the 1930s she changed her hairstyle and make-up with bewildering rapidity, but as the picture opposite shows, the foundation of her stardom was a matchless profile and a superbly sculptured face improved by teeth capping and rigorous dieting.

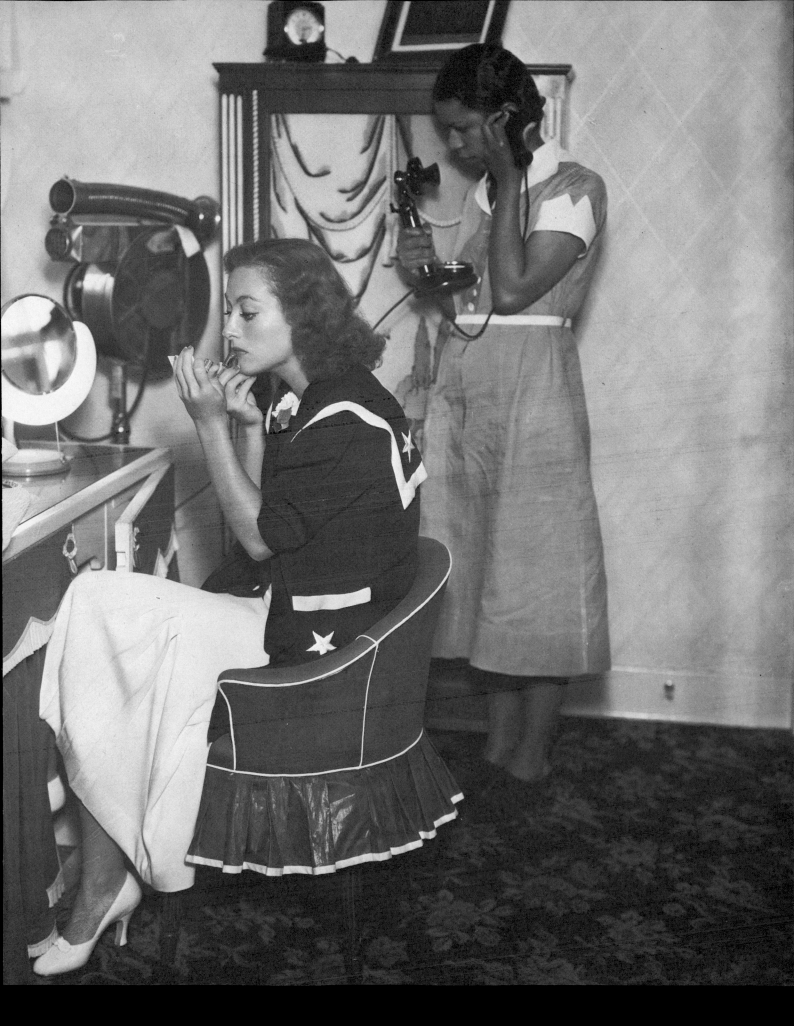

Maybe the novel is self-important, humourless and superficial in its characterization, but if so it was precisely this weakness that made it ideal plot material for the kind of film it was to be.

The search for an actress to play Scarlett was a massively organized publicity stunt during which luminaries from Tallulah Bankhead to Joan Crawford were auditioned. The public had to be made to see that this was *the* great American film and casting Scarlett O'Hara had to be a sacred task.

After *Wuthering Heights*, *The Charge of the Light Brigade*, and so on the movie-makers unconsciously realized that they should be making films reflecting a vision of America such as *It Happened One Night* instead of ransacking English literature and history. It was the American film industry that had the self-confidence to celebrate its own stories and where better to start than with *Gone with the Wind*. It was not by any means the first movie self-consciously to examine the history of the United States, but it was certainly going to be the biggest and best.

There was never any doubt that Gable would play Rhett Butler. His blatant masculinity made the part extraordinarily right for him. Producer David O. Selznick thought so, and he made the decisions. Gable feared that the film would end up Scarlett's rather than Rhett Butler's. Certainly Selznick was primarily aiming the film at women. He sent one of his famous memos to one of his publicists . . . 'I assume you know that the costumes of *Gone with the Wind* are the basis of at least fifty per cent of fashions at this present moment, and I am

Below left: Joan Crawford and Dorothy Sebastian demonstrate their ability to handle life-saving equipment; and right: stepping out with Fred Astaire.

sure the whole business of the return to corsets is due to *Wind*. All of this is trivial and laughable in a world shaken by war, but women being what they are, I think it could make for excellent publicity.'

By contrast, his memos to Gable were nagging and critical. Had Gable got the accent right? The walk? Gable mainly ignored the advice. He could afford to, after all he *was* Rhett Butler.

'Clark is a very nice fellow, but a very suspicious one, and very quickly and not infrequently gets the notion in his head that people are taking advantage of him,' wrote Selznick, and to Carole Lombard he defended himself: 'All through the picture he was frank in expressing his suspicions that I intended to do him in, and I kept pleading with him to wait until the picture was finished and then tell me his opinion.'

Gable's opinion, long after, when he expressed it to Niven, was that he had not come out of *Gone with the Wind* as well as he had intended. 'But – what the hell!'

Joan Crawford with Franchot Tone, her second husband, accompanied by Barbara Stanwyck and her second husband Robert Taylor. Tone was involved in one of the most celebrated Hollywood nightclub punch-ups, with B-movie-star Tom Neal.

The death of Carole Lombard in 1942 was a blow from which he never really recovered. After the war neither he nor his producers knew what kind of movies he should be in. His last was probably his best: *The Misfits* (1961) for John Huston, with Montgomery Clift and a Marilyn Monroe whose temperament added days to the shooting and, said some, took years off Gable's life.

In *The Misfits*, which was written by Arthur Miller, then Monroe's husband, he played a cowboy, a dinosaur, a relic, the last of a breed. He was too, by then, one of the very last of his kind in Hollywood. He was gruffly proud of the Oscar he won for *It Happened One Night*. But it is typical of him that he should have told Niven: 'It has no balls.'

As David Niven has said: 'Gable had enough for both of them.'

Niven was not an intimate of Clark Gable's, but they respected each other's professionalism. For Niven, Gable was the king, *the* super star with the sort of charisma he would never have. He studied Gable and learned from him and Gable's career helped Niven to know what he wanted to do and where he ought to be going.

For Niven was not yet a star. After *The Prisoner of Zenda* he was still at the mercy of the whims of the producers. The Hollywood

Opposite: David Niven takes careful aim.
Below: Vivien Leigh, Laurence Olivier, Marilyn Monroe and her playwright husband Arthur Miller pictured during the making of The Prince and the Showgirl *(1957) in which Monroe and Olivier starred. Olivier also directed, which may account for the careworn expression on his face.*

obsession with the British persisted and he had parts in such movies as *Four Men and a Prayer* (1938), directed by John Ford, in which he was one of the four sons who investigate why their father, Colonel C. Aubrey Smith, was cashiered and discover who framed him. Despite the Irish presence of John Ford as director it was very British, as was *The Dawn Patrol* (1938) a remake of the 1930 film, directed by Niven's friend Edmund Goulding, which celebrated the Royal Flying Corps' achievement in World War I.

The British stiff upper lip might well seem to have contracted rigor mortis, but in *Wuthering Heights* (1939) at least Niven was allowed some room for character development. His performance as Edgar Linton stands up well against the likes of Laurence Olivier having a wonderful time as Heathcliff.

The New York Times, in fact, wrote: 'The Lintons, so pallid, so namby-pamby in the novel, have been more charitably reflected in the picture. David Niven's Edgar, Geraldine Fitzgerald's Isabella are dignified and poignant characterizations of young people whose tragedy was not in being weak themselves, but in being weaker than the abnormal pair whose destinies involved their destruction.'

David Niven was singularly proud of that review, especially as his name was coupled for praise with Geraldine Fitzgerald's, whose work he much admired.

After *Wuthering Heights*, the Quivering Depths? So it would seem for his next movie, in which he was teamed with Ginger Rogers and which had the catchpenny title of *Bachelor Mother* (1939). In fact, it was a warm, light-hearted comedy about an abandoned baby and a shopgirl (Ginger Rogers) being mistaken for its mother not only by the store tycoon's playboy son (Niven) but by all and sundry.

Scripted by Norman Krasna and directed by Garson Kanin it put David Niven's name above the title with Rogers and got him some good reviews for being, what he said came naturally: a playboy.

The London *News Chronicle* said: 'Niven is unbeatable at this sort of romantic comedy.' *The New York Times* chuckled: 'This is the way farce should be handled, with just enough conviction to season its extravagances.'

But it was the London *Observer* which made the important point: 'If Ronald Colman should ever contemplate retirement, which heaven postpone, Mr Niven would seem to be his legitimate successor.'

David Niven kept the cutting of that review, feeling the irony of it deeply. He knew that, originally, he had been brought in to replace Colman as a Goldwyn protégé.

'It seemed as though we were expected to be rivals. But how could we be? He was one of my very best friends.'

It was, though, always useful to Sam Goldwyn to pretend a rivalry existed, a little paranoia, a little fear, these were just what actors needed to keep them to heel.

A War to Fight

It is one of those 'incredible' facts from which the cartoonist Ripley earned a good living during the 1930s with his series 'Believe It Or Not' that Sam Goldwyn had once been apprenticed to a blacksmith in England. At the turn of the century when, aged twelve, he had been *en route* from Poland to America he had stopped off in Britain for four years. Whether or not he could hot-shoe a horse as efficiently as he claimed in late-night conversation, he never had to prove. It certainly gave force to his claim often made when financial disaster threatened: 'I can always work with these,' holding aloft a pair of broad, spatulate hands. Certainly David Niven felt that, on occasion,

Former blacksmith makes good. Below left: Sam Goldwyn, and on the right cutting a dapper figure with his wife on board the liner SS Leviathan.

123

Left: The spoils of Hollywood wars. Mr and Mrs Sam Goldwyn pose for the photographer on the steps of their Hollywood home. Below left: Goldwyn with his second wife, Frances Howard and right: With D. W. Griffith.

Left: Sam Goldwyn (centre) after a 1938 conference in London with Alexander Korda, Mary Pickford and Douglas Fairbanks Jr over the future of United Artists. Douglas Fairbanks is standing behind Goldwyn and Lady Sylvia Ashley, Fairbanks's third wife who later married Clark Gable. On the extreme right is Oscar Deutsch, a powerful figure in British cinema in the 1930s.
Below: Sam Goldwyn with Mr and Mrs Jack Warner.

Goldwyn was using him as an anvil. The hammer of Goldwyn's personality was felt especially fiercely at option time, when contracts were renewed.

Yet Goldwyn's confidence in Niven must have been growing through these years; the 'loan-outs' to other companies, in reality getting them to train Niven, had paid off. Niven had, as he said, 'done my studying in public and been paid handsomely for having done so.'

In 1939, Niven made a comedy called *Eternally Yours*, directed by Tay Garnett, in which he played a hypnotist bent on putting Loretta Young under his spell. It was eminently forgettable, but there followed two rather good films made for Goldwyn: *The Real Glory* (1939). directed by Henry Hathaway, and *Raffles* (1939). In *The Real Glory*, Niven's own heroics were played well behind Gary Cooper's in a story of revolution in the Philippines. Said the London *New Statesman*: 'With Gary Cooper at his most attractive, David Niven and

Gary Cooper relaxes in a hammock and studies a script. Niven co-starred with Cooper and Andrea Leeds in The Real Glory *(1939), directed by Harry Hathaway, a rollicking adventure set in the Philippines. Niven died heroically in the final reel.*

Andrea Leeds looking charming, the film is recommended to adolescents of all ages.' David Niven 'sparkling in the background', commented *The Spectator*.

Raffles was another gesture in the direction of evoking English Edwardian manners. Written by E. W. Hornung, the original stories on which the film was based, it concerned the adventures of a great British cricketer who was also a gentleman burglar. Raffles took advantage of his social position to case the houses he was planning to rob.

Hornung was the brother-in-law of Arthur Conan Doyle, the creator of Sherlock Holmes. Doyle was strongly disapproving of Raffles, even though our hero had more than a touch of Robin Hood about him. Niven told me that secretly he had always hoped he might play Sherlock Holmes on film some day. This was, sadly, a vain hope as Basil Rathbone and Nigel Bruce had created the definitive screen versions of Holmes and Watson.

Gary Cooper and his wife, who is wearing a rather alarming hat. However, even this confection would have had difficulty competing with Gloria Swanson's headgear, one particularly famous example of which was adorned with flashing lightbulbs.

Raffles was directed by William Wyler and Sam Wood. Wood fell ill half-way through. Although Raffles was a role that Niven had long coveted, he was not happy with the English accent he adopted. 'I always felt it sounded too much like an English butler's. That's because English butlers – like British themes – were very much in vogue with the stars in those days. So, I seemed to pick up the tones of whichever butler had served me at whichever party I had been to the night before. A kind of vocal hangover to match the real one!'

Raffles was a box office success for Niven, even though most critics were unkind. *The New York Times*, however, was very generous, it had always had a soft spot for Niven: 'Mr Niven makes the game worth playing and the film worth seeing. His Raffles is one of the nicest tributes to burglary we have seen in many a year.'

Sam Goldwyn had realized how important to Niven the film would be and had dangled the prospect of it in front of him like a carrot in order that Niven would renew his contract. Worse, and very naïvely, Goldwyn had hired a man clad in white tie and tails to follow Niven around and be seen having his photograph taken by a studio stills photographer.

'It was', Niven has written, 'a ploy to get me to rush off and sign the Goldwyn offer.'

Niven signed, of course, and his Hollywood future seemed assured. For the first time, he felt he was really being pampered by Goldwyn.

Below left: Mr and Mrs Arthur Conan Doyle are escorted around the set of Rosita *(1923) by Mary Pickford and Douglas Fairbanks. Rosita was one of Pickford's determined attempts to shrug off the 'Little Mary' image and was a lavish production for which she imported director Ernst Lubitsch from Germany for his first American film.*

Below right: David Niven tries some tentative typing on the set of The Toast of New Orleans *(1950), which co-starred Kathryn Grayson and Mario Lanza.*

David Niven seen here 'dabbling in the kitchen' while he was making Raffles *(1939).*

But fate was to alter Niven's plans as it was to alter so many people's. Those halcyon Hollywood days were to be dramatically cut short. Events on the other side of the world were conspiring to turn dreams to nightmares and fantasy into harsh reality. The outbreak of war between Britain and Germany was not an event which Niven, with his background and education, could ignore. The old school tie, patriotism, the code of a gentleman are all easy concepts to find ludicrous, but for Niven the issues were simple: King and Country were expecting all of him and he must respond.

It would be easy to underestimate the real courage which was now demanded of him, a courage he himself consistently played down. But his self-sacrifice in 1939 was a truly heroic act, a gesture made in cold blood which he knew could mean the end of his career in films.

129

His ties with England had loosened over a decade, but now, when it would have been so easy to have ignored them, he felt bound to do the honourable thing and toss his future into the melting pot of war.

There is an old Chinese saying, which may be entirely a Niven invention, which suggests with bleak determinism that, however ordered one's garden, it is yet subject to snows drifting in from unthought of directions.

Niven also called it the Cockroach Syndrome, a name which derives from Billy Wilder's revenge on Charles Boyer. Billy Wilder, before becoming a director, joined Charles Brackett to make a fine writing team. For the film *Hold Back the Dawn* (1941), with Charles Boyer and Olivia de Havilland, they had written a scene in which Boyer, playing a stateless person waiting in a sleazy hotel room for a visa, is reduced by loneliness to talk to a cockroach crawling on a wall. But Boyer would not say the lines. He was a big star; big stars did not talk to cockroaches, it was beneath their dignity.

Wilder and Brackett were so furious that they decided that if Boyer did not want to talk to this insect, they would give the best dialogue in the film to Boyer's co-star, Olivia de Havilland. As a result, Olivia de Havilland was nominated for an Oscar. 'I had no idea that I owed that Academy nomination to a cockroach spurned by Boyer and championed by Wilder . . .' she wrote.

Niven said he often felt like Miss de Havilland, not knowing why certain events had happened but happy to trust to fate.

In going back to England and the war he had the satisfaction at least of making a decision for himself. He had begun to feel too much at other people's mercy. Once again, he was at least temporarily back in control. In a way he was playing truant or, better still, going to another school.

Sam Goldwyn was not amused and was not fooled by a phoney cable Niven sent himself, requesting his return to England for war service. Reluctantly, he put Niven on contract suspension until such time as the war would be over. Frances, Goldwyn's wife, told Niven afterwards that he had always kept a photograph of his prodigal actor on his desk.

What probably irked Goldwyn more than anything was that Niven's leaving for England was a *fait accompli*. All through his business life he had been the one to make the moves, as when he phoned Darryl F. Zanuck and said: 'Darryl, you and I have a problem.' So what was this mutual problem? 'You have Tyrone Power – and I want him.'

Goldwyn had been out-manoeuvred by Niven, but at least it was nothing less than a world war. He had the grace and humour to tell Niven: 'I'll cable Hitler and ask him to shoot around you.'

'I wouldn't have put it past him either,' Niven was later to recall. 'You know Sam spoke in a very light, near-falsetto voice, but there

Olivia de Havilland, sister of Joan Fontaine. For much of her time at Warners in the 1930s she was the demure foil for a swashbuckling Errol Flynn in a series of classic actioners, the first of which was Captain Blood *(1935). Flynn fell for her, but she sensibly resisted him, later commenting, I'm not going to regret that – it could have ruined my life'. In the 1940s she spread her wings as an actress, winning Best Actress Oscars for her performances in* To Each His Own *(1946) and* The Heiress *(1948).*

was nobody more down-to-earth when it came to looking after his assets. And I was one of his assets.'

Niven had private reasons for wanting to do his bit for England. There was a debt of honour to his own father killed during the first war, and there was the irony of all those mock heroic roles in movies with stories from British history. His Englishness had been a passport to work and social success in Hollywood; now that debt too was called in.

There was nothing for the majority of the actors who made up Hollywood's British colony to feel guilty about. Most of them were too old for service in the armed forces. Niven was only twenty-nine.

How Niven survived the many parties that were given to say farewell to him he never knew. He was surprised at how fervently people he had thought of as strangers would say goodbye to him. They realized what he was doing and were half envious and half thankful that he, not they, was to be sacrificed.

George Raft, the star whose feral dapperness had sustained him throughout his cinematic life, came along to one of those last-time parties to pay his tribute and Jack L. Warner personally rang Niven to wish him *bon voyage*.

Warner Brothers, Warner's studio, had been consistently on the side of Roosevelt during the Depression era, on the side of good

citizenship. Warner was also aware that the rise of the Nazi Party in Germany was a menace, and, at the same time, box office. Warner Brothers' films about the Nazis told audiences truths they did not want to know about the evil that threatened them and at the same time made it all palatable.

'At least you're doing something about it,' Jack L. Warner told David Niven.

Niven records no such fond farewell from Errol Flynn, though doubtless there was one. Flynn's own heroism was later to be mythologized by Hollywood and exaggerated enormously. After the war he sported a chestful of medals, though for what they were awarded no one ever knew.

Flynn was to star as the hero of several of the American war movies which were Hollywood's contribution to morale after the United

Opposite: Niven always looked good in uniform. This photograph was taken during the filming of The Dawn Patrol *(1938), a World War I flying drama executed in the best British stiff upper lip tradition and directed by one of Niven's closest friends Edmund Goulding.*
Above: In his element. George Raft gets to know the Windmill Girls on a 1948 visit to London.

Jack L. Warner and Louis B. Mayer at a party held at the Trocadero. Warner tried to ape the antique collecting passion displayed by William Randolph Hearst, to the extent that a wag nicknamed his house San Simeonette. Errol Flynn called him 'Sporting Blood'. Warner himself most unsportingly described Bette Davis as being about 'as sexy as Slim Summerville'.

States declared war. But at first, with Britain standing alone after the fall of France, the war itself must have seemed like the ultimate scenario for all those movies extolling British virtues and courage which Hollywood had been making throughout the thirties. Propaganda on behalf of Britain had been implicit in all those films, glorifying the British way of life, and American audiences had been unconsciously prepared to sympathize with beleaguered Britain.

In fact sentiment was not the main motive: many movies had British themes, because Britain was far and away the biggest market in Europe for Hollywood's outpourings. Whatever the reason, Hollywood played no small part in making America pro-British and for this Britain was duly thankful. Certainly Hollywood adopted on the screen, if not in reality, the basic British ideals, the sort of public school code with which Niven was so familiar. Loyalty, the supreme virtue, but also the importance of the individual and the individual's healthy disrespect for authority.

So, in a way, the war to which Niven went had been rehearsed in the movies. The good guys were the underdogs besieged, but defiant. The bad guys were the ridiculous strutting dictators. For a moment in Hollywood, Niven was the good guy, a knight in shining armour, even though a few people sneered. Britain would not see him in this light, but Niven was not to know that as he set out for Europe. As he said later, all he did know was that he was 'shit scared'.

A New Role

Raymond Chandler wrote in *The Little Sister* about a certain kind of Hollywood movie: 'One of those glass-and-chromium deals where everybody smiled too much and talked too much and knew it. The women were always going up a long, curving staircase to change their clothes. The men were always taking monogrammed cigarettes out of expensive cases and snapping expensive lighters at each other. And the help was round-shouldered from carrying trays with drinks across the terrace to a swimming pool about the size of Lake Huron but a lot neater.'

Niven with his first wife Primula and their son David Jr. Primula died tragically in 1946 after falling down a flight of stairs while playing 'Sardines' at the home of Tyrone Power.

Left: David Niven and Primmie at the Stork Club, New York and below sorting out photographs taken while Niven was in the Army.
Opposite: Niven at the pool-side with his two sons David (left) and Jamie, shortly after Primmie's death.

Deliberate or not, that was the image most people had, not just of Hollywood movies but of Hollywood society. Hollywood was one of the first instances of an industry setting out to make for itself an artificial but potent myth. Talented artificers had been working on the idea of Hollywood since its early days as the film capital of the world. The mask of glamour may seem in retrospect to have been made of the flimsiest gauze, but it served to distract and bamboozle both then and now.

Although Chandler despised the phoneyness of the place, even though he was one of those makers of the mask, he realized how powerful was the hold Hollywood had on the imagination of millions of outsiders and, more strangely, on the people who lived behind the mask. He once told me: 'There's nobody believes in Hollywood more than one who lives there. You think they would see through the tinsel. But for them it's the real thing, the real tinsel!

Niven with David Jr, who followed in his father's footsteps and is now a highly successful film producer.

'Hollywood was one of the few places on earth which is, of itself, a centre of worship; it became over the years a shrine of Mecca-like proportions, to which the faithful fans turned their faces every time they went to the cinema or opened a film magazine.'

Fortunately for Niven, he was realist enough to know that once he stepped out of Hollywood into a real world at war he was going to be the target for envy. His motives for returning would be questioned and his seriousness of purpose would be a subject for suspicion. So when he arrived back in London, he was not given a hero's welcome.

It was not so much that he was a prodigal son to be forgiven and taken into the fold. As he told me, 'People considered me to be the fatted calf grown rich and bloated on movies.' To some it was irritating that his homecoming could not be simply ignored, but whether they liked it or not, David Niven was famous. His picture was everywhere on posters advertising *Dawn Patrol* and *Bachelor Mother*, both being screened in London cinemas. He allowed Sam Goldwyn's press agent to hold a press conference for him at the Odeon, Leicester Square, and on the poster for *Bachelor Mother* the publicity men had added, 'The star who came home to join the RAF'.

It did not matter that what he had actually said at the press conference was that he *hoped* to join the RAF. The press turned on him sneering: 'Hollywood's first recruit.' 'Relax! The Dawn Patrol is here,' 'Niven spurns the army – "It's the RAF for me".'

The result was that the Group Captain who interviewed Niven when he applied to join up was sarcastic about his chances of joining the RAF and he was to experience unpleasantness on other occasions when he met male members of the British public. His desire to join in the defence of what he still thought of as his homeland was rewarded by a slap in the face from many who enjoyed letting David Niven, the Hollywood star, know that he was now just one more would-be recruit. 'I felt I was back in those early days in Hollywood when it was so difficult to get work.'

For Hollywood, or what the public imagined it to be, had travelled with him like an aura he could not shrug off. There was a sense of puzzlement that he had escaped from life's typecasting – that of elegant blade – to join in the rough-and-tumble of the real world. The stars should stay in their courses or risk being pulled down.

But Niven's talent for making friends once again stood him in good stead. One of them pulled strings so that, after several weeks of miserably living in a vacuum, he joined the Second Battalion of the Rifle Brigade as a second lieutenant. After being given the pip he had got his pips!

Before the Battle of Britain, when German planes tried to bomb the islands into submission, there was a period of what was called 'the phoney war'. Niven was given the job of teaching men to drive trucks, but in his spare time was drawn into London's still active, social life. It was during these months that he met Winston Churchill, shortly to become Prime Minister.

Churchill was aware of who Niven was and had always enjoyed Hollywood's glitter. Indeed, he was the kind of leader who might well have come straight from a Hollywood historical epic, such as *Lady Hamilton* (1942) starring Laurence Olivier and Vivien Leigh. Churchill adored this kind of fanciful depiction of great characters from Britain's history. At least he appreciated Niven's sacrifice or so Niven recorded in *The Moon's a Balloon*: 'Young man, you did a very fine thing to give up a most promising career to fight for your country.' Then he added: 'Mark you, had you not done so – it would have been despicable!'

It was a marvellous exit line from a conversation which certainly delighted David Niven and made up for all those sneers. The headmaster of Britain had given his approval of a new boy's behaviour.

It was also around this time that Niven met and married Primula, a cypher clerk at the RAF Reconnaissance Squadron at Heston, outside London. It was, as he said later, without the slightest trace of coyness, love at first sight. Women had always been a highly necessary part of Niven's life, but though he enjoyed sex for its own sake, he was also extraordinarily romantic. He had sown plenty of wild oats in Hollywood. But Hollywood, and all it meant as substitute family, was a very long way away. So, after a few sexual excursions, it was time to find a partner who could give him security and support. Niven told me that settling down for him meant children, a family. 'I'm not a dynasty man, but it is good to see the line carried on.'

Primula was Primula Rollo, niece of the 12th Lord Rollo, and by her Niven was to father two sons; David Niven Junior and Jamie. While Niven, like so many soldiers, sought permanence, Britain was facing defeat. Daily, aerial fights were taking place in the skies which were to decide if anyone had a future.

Niven himself had been seconded to a unit which had just been formed, crack troops who were trained for the toughest combat: the commandos. He was to start as major, and end as colonel.

Niven was always reticent about his wartime exploits, but he seems to have been involved in the 1942 raid on Dieppe and the Normandy landings. 'Those days are past; better forget 'em. Let's hope they never happen again.'

His face, though, was famous enough not to be forgotten and he was called on to speak at meetings to raise National Savings, to boost morale that might be thought to be 'flagging'.

Even more useful to the war effort were his acting talents. Niven was to go back to the movies, but all for 'the war effort'.

It is a curious paradox that the 1942 film, *The First of the Few*, called *Spitfire* in the United States, directed by Leslie Howard, should have extolled the joys of combat as a member of the Royal

Air Force. He had not been allowed to join the RAF in real life, but there was always the movies.

Leslie Howard, also the film's star, was blond and blue-eyed, the son of Hungarian immigrants to London. Yet despite these ethnic origins, he seemed the archetypal diffident English gentleman, an amateur with a professional touch. Of an easy amiability until roused, Howard had met Niven first in Hollywood when he came to make *Gone with the Wind*. He had been a marvellous Professor Higgins in George Bernard Shaw's *Pygmalion* (1938) and was a splendid Scarlet Pimpernel in the film of that name and, then, *Pimpernel Smith*. In the first he was smuggling French aristos out of Revolutionary France, while in the second he was doing the same thing with refugees from the Nazi terror.

A complex man, despite the seeming simplicity of his manner, Niven recalled: 'I never really got to know how his mind worked. There was so much going on behind that charming façade.'

British stars Greer Garson, Leslie Howard, Vivien Leigh, Brian Aherne, Ronald Colman and Basil Rathbone make a wartime radio broadcast for NBC. Early in 1943, while flying from Portugal to London, Leslie Howard's aircraft was shot down by German fighters. Churchill was returning from his Algiers conference that day, and the Germans thought that he was on the same aircraft.

141

He died in 1943 in an air crash and it seems likely that the plane he was in was shot down by the Germans because they believed it was carrying Winston Churchill.

Niven's role in *The First of the Few* was that of Geoffrey Crisp, who was an amalgam of all Mitchell's test pilots. It was a role tailor-made for Niven's brand of flip gallantry and the reviews expressed the critics' satisfaction with his performance. The *Scotsman* thought it was one of the best things he had ever done, while the *Observer* said: 'Oddly enough, since Mitchell (the inventor of the Spitfire played in the film by Leslie Howard) was a real man and Crisp is merely a symposium of test pilots, an imaginary creation, it is Mitchell who seems the figment, Crisp the flesh-and-blood character. David Niven's flippant assurance is just right here. The real-life story is the more real for his imagined presence; he gives the rather abstracted film a body.'

There was no lull in Niven's service duties and he did not make another film until 1944.

Hollywood at war: Clark Gable leans nonchalantly on the waist gun of a United States Auxiliary Air Force bomber.

Then came *The Way Ahead* (1944), directed by Carol Reed. It developed from an Army film service short, *The New Lot*, commissioned to show how civilians adjusted to service life. The Adjutant General was so impressed with the result that he suggested expanding it into a feature film – the Army's answer to *In Which We Serve*.

Niven himself played the part of a young officer who, having returned from Dunkirk, had the job of licking the recruited combatants into military shape. *The New York Times* said of his performance: 'In one scene, wherein he dresses down the trainee, he accomplishes a truly heart-disturbing soldier's monologue.'

Of course, when America entered the war, Hollywood also went to war and Niven was by no means the only star who, at least on the silver screen, beat Hitler more or less single-handed. Clark Gable appeared as a major in a bombing squadron and James Stewart also looked excellent in uniform. With the war nearly won, Niven became very nervous about his future in cinema and even if he was to have one at all. As he wrote: 'Six months is too long for an actor to be out of business – six years is almost certain disaster.' So when the European conflict ceased and he sent a telegram to Sam Goldwyn to announce his availability he did not know what the reply would be. 'Knowing Sam it could have been anything. Like "How could you do this war to me?" to a simpler "Get stuffed!"'

Below left: Raising the flag of MGM. No one was more patriotic than Hollywood's movie moguls, most of whom were immigrants from Europe.
Below right: In the early 1930s the fashion was for anti-war films like The Eagle and the Hawk *(1933), which starred Fredric March and Gary Grant. Here an uncharacteristically soberly dressed Jean Harlow visits Franchot Tone and Cary Grant on the set.*

Left and below: Marlene Dietrich visiting troops during World War II. In 1942, her film career was in the doldrums after a run of indifferent films at Universal. She solved the problem by undertaking a gruelling tour of duty entertaining the troops, for which she was awarded the Medal of Freedom.

As it was, Goldwyn's reply from a Hollywood which had not seen Niven for six years was not unwelcoming. There was to be a new five-year contract at what seemed more advantageous terms. And Niven's first film under this contract was to be on 'loan out' to the distinguished producers-directors-screenwriters Michael Powell and Emeric Pressburger.

Powell and Pressburger had a production company called The Archers and were often right on target with projects which were always original in theme and treatment.

The film to star David Niven was to be *A Matter of Life and Death* (1946), which was known as *Stairway to Heaven* in the United States. It was the first film to be chosen for the Royal Film Performance and was an allegory.

Niven played the role of Peter Carter, a bomber pilot who survives his plane's crash in England and is then, he believes, summoned to Heaven, where a debate between American isolationism, personified by Raymond Massey, and Roger Livesey ensues as to whether Carter ought to live. Love, in the person of the American service girl (Kim Hunter), finds a way and Peter Carter is restored to life. It was

A highlight of Dietrich's wartime act was a rendition of 'Lili Marlene', a haunting song as popular with the Allies' fighting men as the German troops. After the war she sang it in concert appearances all over the world.

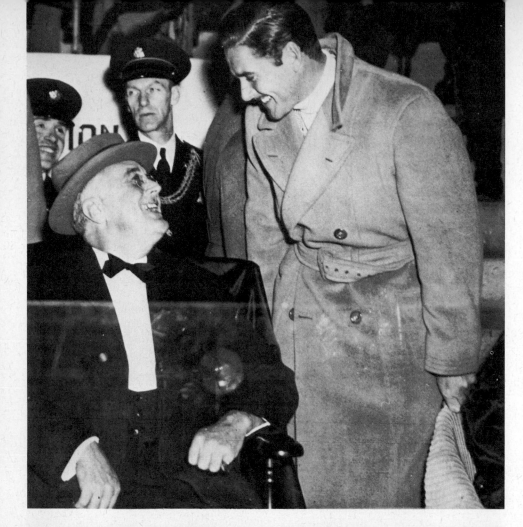

Left: Franklin D. Roosevelt with Errol Flynn, the man who won the war singlehanded on celluloid in films like Objective Burma (1945), in which he cleared Burma of the Japanese.

Below left: James Stewart, seen here with Henry Fonda at the club run by the Hollywood character Slapsy Maxie Rosenbloom, had a distinguished war record. He flew bombing missions over Germany and remains one of the highest-ranking officers in the United States Auxiliary Air Force.

Below right: Vice President Harry Truman tickles the ivories and admires Lauren Bacall's legs at the National Press Club canteen, October 1945.

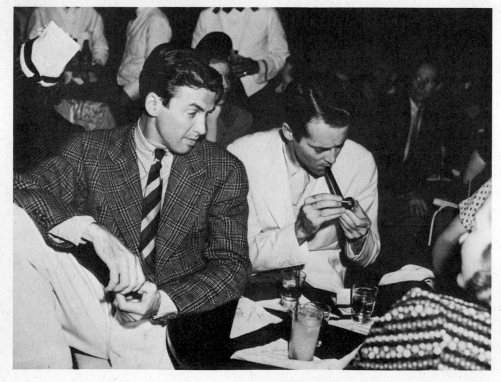

accused by some of being anti-British, and by others of being anti-American, but Niven himself got some of the best critical notices of his career.

Michael Powell said of David Niven: 'I had always admired his work. He seemed, so often, so much better than the material which he was in. I thought he would be marvellous as Peter Carter, because despite all that surface gallantry there is a sense of underlying strain which is only really perceived by the keen onlooker. It's what always gives his performances that extra dimension of reality. Whatever you think about the film now, I think *he* was quite exceptional.'

Then it was time for Niven to return to Hollywood, but not before the British tax man had grabbed everything of Niven's he could lay hands on. His leaving, therefore, was as unfriendly as his welcome had been six years earlier. He gave a farewell party at Claridges,

Loretta Young and James Stewart. Young was a durable star who made her good looks and limited talent go a long way. Underneath the glamour she was a tough professional, nicknamed 'the Steel Butterfly' by her first husband Grant Withers. She made her screen debut as a fourteen-year-old extra in The Only Way *(1926), and twenty years later, when her career was on the slide, won an Oscar for her performance in* The Farmer's Daughter *(1947).*

welcomed all whom he felt had been his friends, but refused to invite those he felt had been unkind to him. It is one of the rare instances in which David Niven made judgements about whom he considered worth calling friends.

In any case, Niven was a very much more mature man. He was now responsible for a wife and two small sons. His future was uncertain. He had, he once told me, been tempted to stay in England to work for British movies. In fact, the Rank Organization had dangled the carrot of a contract ahead of him if he would only stay and work at their Pinewood Studios. But he felt he had to get back to Hollywood, as if to face an old school after a long, if rackety, vacation. Irritation with its way of life might well come later. But it was the world he knew and he felt at home in Hollywood. It was time to find out how much things had changed, and whether there was still a place for him in the Californian sun.

David Niven and his wife greet J. Arthur Rank, Britain's answer to Louis B. Mayer. Rank emerged from World War II at the head of an extremely powerful film empire, but he then fatally overreached himself in attempting to take on the Americans in their own market.

Return of the Warrior

Hollywood had changed and so had Niven. Tinseltown glamour looked threadbare beneath the glare of the lights. The studios were still pumping out escapist entertainment, but more purposefully and with no pretence that anyone was trying to make anything more elevated than money.

Niven once recalled that in the 1930s Hollywood could be a very menacing place, but the parties and the social whirl tended to disguise the reality. Now, though, the naked rapacity beneath the surface glitter was more blatant. It was as though the war had made people less naïve, though not necessarily more mature. Certainly, David Niven did not feel as at ease in postwar Hollywood despite the huge welcome he received. There was a grand homecoming party at which many of Hollywood's most important and influential citizens greeted him as a lamb returning to the fold.

Niven's unease was in part physical. He had not properly recovered from the bronchial pneumonia he had contracted. More importantly, he started off, from the point of view of his career, very much on the

MGM boasted, with some justification, that it was 'the studio with more stars than there are in heaven'. This was their 1949 line up (not all the stars, however, were available at the time the photograph was taken): Left to right: FIRST ROW: Lionel Barrymore, June Allyson, Leon Ames, Fred Astaire, Edward Arnold, Lassie, Mary Astor, Ethel Barrymore, Spring Byington, James Craig, Arlene Dahl. SECOND ROW: Gloria De Haven, Tom Drake, Jimmy Durante, Vera-Ellen, Errol Flynn, Clark Gable, Ava Gardner, Judy Garland, Betty Garrett, Edmund Gwenn, Kathryn Grayson, Van Heflin. THIRD ROW: Katharine Hepburn, John Hodiak, Claude Jarman, Jr, Van Johnson, Jennifer Jones, Louis Jourdan, Howard Keel, Gene Kelly, Christopher Kent, Angela Lansbury, Mario Lanza, Janet Leigh. FOURTH ROW: Peter Lawford, Jeanette MacDonald, Ann Miller, Ricardo Montalban, Jules Munshin, George Murphy, Reginald Owen, Walter Pigdeon, Jane Powell, Ginger Rogers, Frank Sinatra, Red Skelton. FIFTH ROW: Alexis Smith, Ann Sothern, J. Carrol Naish, Dean Stockwell, Lewis Stone, Clinton Sundberg, Robert Taylor, Audrey Totter, Spencer Tracy, Esther Williams, Keenan Wynn.

Above left: A warm welcome from a Red Cross worker on a New York pier as David Niven returns to America.
Above right: At his home in Pacific Pallisades, known as The Pink House. It had been built some forty years before by Vicki Baum, author of Grand Hotel.
Left: A welcome back to Hollywood from Sam Goldwyn and Hedda Hopper, but the great days of the studios were drawing to a close.
Opposite: The garden of the Pink House, which boasted magnificent views of the Pacific; and the drawing-room.

wrong foot. The movie on which he started work in 1946 was evidence of Goldwyn's complete misunderstanding about the kind of star he now had in David Niven. It says a good deal for Niven's basic toughness that he was able to survive such poor-quality movies as he was now asked to act in. His private word for them was 'stinkers'; they could well have been designed with the sole idea of dragging Niven down as an actor.

Surprisingly, Niven went up in public esteem rather than down. To begin with, absence had made the heart grow fonder and, in those six years away from film making, instead of being forgotten, his image seems to have flourished in the public's mind. It was good that it had, for there was nothing now to nourish it.

The first of a string of mediocre films was *The Perfect Marriage* (1946), directed by Lewis Allen, in which he co-starred with Loretta Young. It was about a ten-year relationship which is about to collapse

Fred Astaire with his sister Adèle (left), an incomparable dance team in the 1920s. Their first big success was in a 1922 show specially written for them, For Goodness Sake, *which was on Broadway and in the West End. Their last big hit was the 1931* The Band Wagon, *after which Adèle married into the British aristocracy.*

Elegant and relaxed as ever, Fred Astaire entertains his young son Fred Jr on the set of MGM's Easter Parade *(1948). Astaire described his work with Judy Garland on that film as 'one of the high spots' of his career.*

when shared memories and affection save it. Niven hardly remembered it when I mentioned it to him years later, but when the horror of it flooded back into his consciousness, I remember he groaned quietly.

Goldwyn had insisted that Niven take the role, as indeed he did with the next movie, *Magnificent Doll*, also made in 1946 and directed by Frank Borzage. Niven described this as 'gibberish'. It was a historical drama in which he played Aaron Burr, Jefferson's vice-president, who killed a rival in a duel. Ginger Rogers played Dolly Payne, a girl who becomes involved with Burr. 'She would have been better off with Fred Astaire rather than me,' said Niven.

The Other Love (1947), in which Niven played the gallant doctor of a Swiss sanatorium who falls in love and marries concert pianist

Tyrone Power with Linda Christian in Venice while Power was on location filming for Prince of Foxes *(1949), a handsome costume epic directed by Henry King and featuring a bravura performance by Orson Welles as Cesare Borgia. Power and Christian were married shortly after he completed the film. A protegé of Darryl F. Zanuck, the devastatingly handsome Power was at his best as a romantic swashbuckler in* The Mark of Zorro *(1940) and* The Black Swan *(1942).*

Barbara Stanwyck, was not much better. Niven did his best, but the movie, thanks to the director André de Toth, was sickly sentimental and Barbara Stanwyck was quite out of sympathy with her role.

David Niven was naturally worried that whatever confidence the public had in him would rapidly disappear unless he could soon be associated with a success. He had several arguments with Sam Goldwyn, who was making him take on bad roles in bad films, but the blow that knocked him to the ground was a personal one. His adored wife Primmie died in a tragic accident at the age of twenty-five.

It was early in the evening at the home of Tyrone Power. There was a party and people were playing the child's game of 'Sardines'. Primmie opened a door thinking it to be a clothes cupboard. In the dark, she stepped forward and fell down a steep flight of steps into a cellar. She suffered brain damage and never regained consciousness.

Niven told me it was the unexpectedness for one thing that shook him. 'It's always the same, you don't like the way someone you love passes away. What we don't like, really, is the passing at all. But it was not being prepared for it which was so awful. It was so sudden. It was like being at war again; it happened with a friend who never

came back. You expected it then. But not in peacetime, not like this. In the midst of life we are in death. That was certainly true for me all right.'

His grief hit him hardest after some weeks had elapsed. In despair, he tried to forget the emptiness in his emotional life in a mindless gaiety. 'It all affected me sexually,' he told me, 'I was insatiable. No woman was safe. It was no disrespect or lack of love for Primmie – it's just that I was trying to get something out of my system that was better out than in. I believe I was very ill in a sexual kind of way.'

Work was itself a kind of therapy and he had a role in a film which Goldwyn was himself producing. Ironically in the circumstances, it was a light comedy called *The Bishop's Wife* (1947) and Niven needed all his courage to bring it off. It was not smooth going in any case. Goldwyn saw the first 'rushes' and hated them. He fired the director, had the script rewritten and the sets rebuilt. Goldwyn may have been crude and even ridiculous, but he was no fool, and the resulting film, directed by Henry Koster, was a success, at least commercially. It was Niven's second Royal Film Performance, but that did not prevent it being mauled by the critics.

Tyrone Power at a Madison Square Garden boxing match. After the war he tried manfully to extend his range beyond that encompassed by a flickering sword and a flashing grin, notably as an alcoholic in Edmund Goulding's Nightmare Alley *(1947). At the end of his career he returned to the kind of vehicle which had made him famous and died of a heart attack while filming a duel with George Sanders in King Vidor's* Solomon and Sheba *(1959). There was a double irony in his death, as Sanders and Power had fought a duel twenty years before in Lloyds of London* (1935).

It had a memorable cast. Apart from Niven, it starred Loretta Young and Cary Grant, but the film was coated in enough sentiment to make the sweetest tooth ache.

Niven's role was that of an Episcopalian bishop, out of touch with his wife (Loretta Young) and daughter (Karolyn Grimes). Enter an angel called Dudley, played by Cary Grant. Grant's usual urbane sweet exterior cracked on the set in the knowledge that, artistically, the film was not going to be a success and, untypically, he threw several tantrums.

The London *News Chronicle* noted that: 'It is the Protestant comeback to the deadly successful R.C. propaganda of *Going My Way* and *The Bells of St Mary's*. *The Bishop's Wife* surpasses in tastelessness, equals in whimsy and in technique falls well below those crooning parables.' Then it stopped with an afterthought that was a *coup de grâce*: 'It is really quite a monstrous film.'

Monstrous or not, it was a success at the box office. After what had gone before, Niven was happy about this and indeed he claims to have enjoyed making it. The co-writer was the famous American playwright Robert Sherwood – 'and I felt that Sam's predilection for going for respectable literary figures had paid off in the quality of the dialogue.'

He was not to be so happy about his next film, *Bonnie Prince Charlie* (1948), directed by Anthony Kimmins. Niven has recalled many instances of Sam Goldwyn losing that famous temper, but Niven could also lose his when he had to. *Bonnie Prince Charlie* was a prime example of a time when Niven felt he had to fight Goldwyn in order to survive, and fight he did.

Goldwyn had agreed to loan out Niven again, this time to Alexander Korda, the great movie entrepreneur whose ventures were so fraught with problems that he seemed always on the point of shipwreck. Usually it was his backers who suffered while he sailed on to the next project. He was delightful company, cigar ever clenched between his lips, tales being told in that quiet Hungarian-accented voice. My own personal recollection of him was of a man who enveloped you within the warmth of his personality, as though it were a cloak. Somehow or other, he convinced you that you were accomplices in a world that was too secure and safe for its own good.

With movies such as *The Private Life of Henry VIII* (1933), starring Charles Laughton, Korda expressed his fascination with British history. He seemed to want to be more English than English. *Bonnie Prince Charlie* was an attempt to create a Hollywood epic. That was why he needed Niven for the role of the Young Pretender. Niven seemed to Korda to straddle both Hollywood and Britain.

Niven resisted at first, not liking the idea of the movie and feeling hesitant about impersonating such a famous figure as Bonnie Prince Charlie. Goldwyn put him on suspension and Niven had to relent;

David Niven with his second wife Hjördis Tersmeden on their honeymoon.

Left: David Niven and Hjördis shortly after they got married.
Below left: A spot of painting at home.
Below right: Going all out for the smash at a tennis party.

he had put a good deal of money into a home he was building and he had two small boys to educate. Goldwyn bore him no grudge and next time he had dinner with the Goldwyns, Sam was just as affable as he could be. Goldwyn never took his business or his rudeness home with him.

Bonnie Prince Charlie took nearly a year to complete and cost just under a million pounds, no small sum in the postwar austerity year of 1948. Niven recalled: 'There was never a completed screenplay and never at any time during the eight months we were shooting were the writers more than two days ahead of the actors . . . (whenever we actors really started to breathe down the writers' necks, Korda ordered another battle to delay us for a few more days)!'

He wrote after, it all seemed like a bad dream: 'I felt sorry for him, but I felt much sorrier for myself as the Bonnie Prince who would assuredly bear the blame for the impending débâcle. . . .'

Niven had gone blond for the occasion and some critics had great fun with that, comparing his hair unfavourably with Laurence Olivier's, who had gone blond for Hamlet.

One critic noted Niven's 'fugitive charm', but another said that David Niven looked as much at home 'as a goldfish in a haggis'.

It was not, however, all disaster, for it was on the set of *Bonnie Prince Charlie* – in the make-up room, where his flaxen hair was being styled – that he met Hjördis, who was to be his second wife, and that within ten days. She was Swedish, and a quite beautiful model, Niven described it all as a *coup de foudre*.

Next came a stage romance for Goldwyn, called *Enchantment* (1948), directed by Irving Reis, followed by a loan-out for Warner Brothers, *A Kiss in the Dark* (1949), one of Niven's worst films, directed by Delmer Davies. Then came another call from Korda.

This time it was to return to England to make a film of *The Elusive Pimpernel* (1950), a remake and update of *The Scarlet Pimpernel*, which starred Leslie Howard. It was to be made by Michael Powell and Emeric Pressburger, who had made *A Matter of Life and Death*. Niven, however, was not happy about returning to Britain, scene of his recent débâcle with *Bonnie Prince Charlie* and, although he submitted, relations with Goldwyn became even chillier.

The Elusive Pimpernel was another trouble-ridden movie. Michael Powell had wanted to make the story as a musical, but Korda rejected the idea. Powell said: 'It never went right because there were relics of the musical idea still in it. I'd given it a completely different story line but Alex and Samuel Goldwyn wanted a lot of the original story line put back again . . . if you're making a film between Goldwyn and Alex Korda . . . you get ground to powder.'

What with the extensive retakes, the film eventually cost nearly half a million pounds. David Lewin of the *Daily Express* was at a news conference held for Goldwyn and Korda to publicize the film.

David Niven at the Pink House, which was found for him by Douglas Fairbanks Jr.

158

How much, Korda was asked, had he spent on the retakes.

'Two per cent of the cost of the picture,' Korda replied.

'How much did the picture cost?'

Replied Korda: 'One hundred per cent.'

Korda's problem was, as Niven put it later, that he was in the business of exorcism. In his early years as a producer he had had a tough time in Hollywood and had never quite come to terms with it. Now, in his later years, Korda was determined to spend huge amounts of money in making genuine Hollywood epics. It was his image of what Hollywood should be and, in a way, his revenge on Hollywood. *The Elusive Pimpernel* was not a critical success and only a minor success at the box office.

'It must be one of the most expensively dull films we have made in this country for years,' wrote the *Daily Express* film critic. 'David

Alexander Korda with his wife Merle Oberon pictured outside Buckingham Palace after he received his knighthood in 1942. His great days as the undisputed baron of British films were already behind him. In the 1930s the international success of The Private Life of Henry VIII *(1933) and* Rembrandt *(1936) encouraged him into a doomed attempt to rival Hollywood and turn his Denham studios into a British version of MGM.*

159

Salvador Dali paints Laurence Olivier in the title role of Richard III (1954), the last film produced by Alexander Korda.

Niven plays the Scarlet Pimpernel with the sheepish lack of enthusiasm of a tone deaf man called to sing solo in church. His companions lumber through their parts like schoolboys about to go down with mumps.'

The Times worried that 'Film audiences are in danger of forgetting what a really accomplished actor Mr Niven is.'

This last was heartily echoed by Niven, who went back to Hollywood, only to be put into what is called 'a disastrous teenage pot boiler'. This was *A Kiss for Corliss* (1949), in which a grown-up Shirley Temple was his co-star, as a bobby-soxer.

C. A. Lejeune, the film critic of the *Observer*, was driven to rhyme by the ineptness of it all:

'I sometimes think that David Niven
should not take *all* the parts he's given.
While of the art of Shirley Temple
I, for the moment, have had ample.'

Niven had had to work very hard to get where he was, but whether through bad advice, ill judgement or bad luck, he had been given a succession of mediocre films. Niven was a success, a star, but his career was sadly empty of films to be proud of. Insecurity or good nature had allowed him to take on far too many 'easy' roles, which amounted to very little and left a bad taste in his mouth. Should he take some critics' advice and rid himself of Sam Goldwyn?

Humphrey Bogart taking a boat trip in Genoa during a break from filming The Barefoot Contessa *(1954), directed by Joseph L. Mankiewicz and co-starring Ava Gardner and Rosanno Brazzi. The film was a thinly disguised version of the romance between Rita Hayworth and Prince Aly Khan.*

Niven was aware that Goldwyn's choice of movies for him was proving disastrous and he resented being treated as a Goldwyn investment to be loaned out to all and sundry as and when it suited the great man. It was the extras' 'Meat Market' raised to the power of stardom.

Niven had offers of better work if he left Goldwyn and so, with his courage bolstered by these, he sought an interview with Goldwyn. It was short and not noticeably sweet. When it ended, Niven was no longer an employee of Samuel Goldwyn. He felt as though something had been severed; was it a chain or an artery? He found it difficult to decide.

In *The Moon's a Balloon*, Niven remembers that it was Humphrey Bogart who put it all into hideous perspective for him: 'Let's face it, kid – you've blown it! Keep going somehow, mortgage the house, sell the kids, dig a ditch, do anything but for Christ's sake never let them think they've got you running scared because somewhere in somebody's desk is a script that's right for you and when they dig it out – it's you they'll want and nobody else and everything'll be forgotten.'

Niven hoped desperately that Bogart was right.

Out on a Limb

David Niven was now out on his own. The umbilical cord that had tied him to Goldwyn had been cut. He was free, but whether to sink or swim was anybody's guess. The temptation for Niven was to cling to any passing driftwood rather than wait for the life raft. He could not resist the temptation and found himself involved again in the sort of mediocre films he had tried to escape by leaving Goldwyn.

The Toast of New Orleans (1950), directed by Norman Taurog, was the vehicle MGM had chosen to launch their new singing star Mario Lanza, a barrel-chested tenor who died young, bloated by champagne and success. The film also starred Kathryn Grayson and Niven played her manager. It was not a production that Niven took any pleasure in recalling.

Happy Go Lovely, also made in 1950 and directed by Bruce Humberstone, was no better. It was a musical as indigestible as any collapsed *soufflé*, set at the Edinburgh Festival. Niven, who came to Britain to make the film, played a greetings card tycoon who becomes involved with a chorus girl. Though the film was unmemorable, Niven got his best reviews for some time.

Said the *Spectator*: 'Mr David Niven's charm helps enormously to blind one to the picture's defects.' That there were defects, though, was only too obvious.

In a rare venture into American theatre, Niven joined Gloria Swanson in a play called *Nina*. At one performance Miss Swanson's corset snapped during a tender embrace and some inches of whalebone erupted into Niven. Neither he nor Miss Swanson were amused, although the audience was. Niven was not by instinct a stage actor and this attempt to conquer Broadway ended in disaster.

The film offers failed to materialize and Niven began to fear that he had been put on a Hollywood Black List by order of Goldwyn. It was nerve-racking, even frightening to feel so unwanted.

'I could have been wrong, I probably was, but there was a sniff of conspiracy in the air. The word "paranoia" wasn't well known to me at the time, but in my bones I knew what it meant all right!'

Niven was not alone in feeling frightened for the future. Hollywood as a whole was trying to come to terms with the first real rival to cinema: television. No one knew what effect it would have on cinema audiences, but no one was fool enough to believe that everything would go on as before.

The studios' immediate reaction was to look for novelty. New faces, new themes – anything to make television look boring.

A hard row to hoe. David Niven gets down to work in the garden, where he seems to be raising a bumper crop.

This was one good reason why old hands like Niven were being rejected and the sort of movies that he had starred in were being labelled old-fashioned. The studio houses were suddenly unsure of their audience's taste and too many movies were bland compromises, lacking the self-confidence of pre-war Hollywood. One answer, though it proved not to be the right one, was to pretend that things had not changed and deliberately go for the much-loved British Empire story.

So in 1951, we find Niven making *Soldiers Three*, directed by Tay Garnett, an adaptation of stories by Rudyard Kipling which would have done well in 1931 but hardly seemed appropriate two decades and a world war later.

In this film, Niven was joined by two excellent British actors: Stewart Granger and Robert Newton. It was, as he later said, highly agreeable company but the film itself, set in British-ruled India circa

Hjördis gets a coy peck on the forehead from the bristling Trubshawe in 1950, the year he starred in Michael Powell's The Elusive Pimpernel.

163

1890, proved a flop at the box-office. It did include one memorable scene in which Niven has to put on lady's knickers, but it is otherwise utterly forgettable.

There followed *The Lady Say No!* (1951), directed by Frank Ross, a dire movie to which Niven should also have said 'no', and then a return to Britain for *Appointment with Venus* (1951), directed by Ralph Thomas and called *Island Rescue* in the United States. This was a very British story about rescuing a champion cow in calf from a German-occupied Channel Island. Feeling that he could hardly do worse by staying in Hollywood, Niven chanced his arm and took the role of an army major. He thoroughly enjoyed it and *The Times* said:

'It is pleasant to watch Mr Niven going about his work – although that is too stern a word – of being as nonchalant as he is gifted, as gay as he is determined, a twentieth-century Pimpernel with an aristocrat of a cow to snatch from under the noses of the enemy.'

The film was edited by Gerald Thomas, who was to submerge his talent for direction in creating the *Carry On* . . . farces which Niven much admired and in which, he once confessed, he would have liked to have appeared as a guest star.

After *Appointment With Venus* things looked very bleak for Niven. Goldwyn had put it about that he had been fired and this did not help. It just seemed impossible for Niven to find anything which would give his career the lift it so desperately needed. Just when Niven was on the point of giving up, Otto Preminger offered him a role in *The*

Opposite above left: Gloria Swanson holds court. At her feet on the right is Laurence Olivier, with whom she co-starred in an ill-fated British film of 1933, Perfect Understanding, *a quality in short supply during its production in the middle of which her actor husband Michael Farmer was fired and replaced by Olivier.*

Opposite above right: Gloria apes Suzanne Lenglen, winner of the lawn tennis singles and mixed doubles in the 1920 Olympics, on the tennis court.

Opposite below: With her husband the ubiquitous Marquis de la Falaise de Coudraye on the set of Queen Kelly *(1928), a $600,000 folie de grandeur directed by Erich von Stroheim and financed by Swanson's lover, Joseph Kennedy. With no end to its production in sight, Gloria pulled out the plugs – the story goes that she told von Stroheim she had to make a telephone call, left the set and never came back. Swanson later claimed that she was not free of the debt until after she made* Sunset Boulevard *(1950).*

Left: Stewart Granger, Jean Simmons and Niven on the set of Soldiers Three *(1951), Tay Garnett's freewheeling remake of* Gunga Din *(1939).*

Moon Is Blue (1953). Preminger had seen and liked Niven in the stage disaster *Nina*.

Preminger, however, was about as difficult to deal with as Goldwyn. He had a fearsome reputation and would rant and rage on set using sarcasm like a whip. Jean Seberg was one of many actors and actresses who regarded Preminger in the same light as Fay Wray did King Kong. Certainly in Niven's case, though the relationship was not an easy one, it was softened by respect and, ultimately, affection.

The Moon is Blue was based on a mildly risqué Broadway play by F. Hugh Herbert. It was virtually a three-hander and starred, apart from Niven, Maggie McNamara and William Holden, who had just won an Oscar for his performance in *Stalag 17* (1953).

David Niven and Glynis Johns on location for Appointment with Venus *(1951), a charmingly offbeat war story set in the occupied Channel Islands produced by Betty Box and directed by Ralph Thomas.*

Preminger was a shrewd publicist and, innocent though the film looks today, he made much of three taboo words: 'mistress', 'seduce', and 'virgin'. Against all the rules and the disapproval of the Catholic Church he insisted on keeping these words in the script. Things had not changed much since David Selznick had had to plead with the directors of the Production Association for permission to let Rhett Butler say he didn't give a damn in *Gone with the Wind*. Niven himself recalled that in *The Late George Apley* (1946) a girl had to ask Apley what the book he was reading was all about. 'Sex' comes the answer, but that could not be allowed and Apley has to say 'It's all about . . .' and whisper the rest of the sentence. All of which ended up more titillating than the little word itself.

Otto Preminger won his battle, backed by his distributors United Artists. *The Moon is Blue* featured the three naughty words and the publicity was enormous. The film was a box-office success which pleased Holden, who had had a stake in it, and delighted Niven, who had no financial·stake but a reputation to recover. It felt very good to be a star again.

David Niven may not have realized it at the time but something important had happened. He was no longer a Hollywood star – he was an international star. Painfully, accidentally, unremarked,

Below left: Niven with Hedda Hopper. In Bring on the Empty Horses, *Niven wrote of Hopper and Louella Parsons, 'Only Hollywood could have spawned such a couple and only Hollywood, headline-hunting, self-inflating, riddled with fear and insecurity, could have allowed itself to be dominated by them for so long.'*
Below right: With director Otto Preminger while filming Bonjour Tristesse *(1958), in which Niven gave a performance of subtle charm as Jean Seberg's philandering father.*

Niven had abandoned ship just in time. Had he been tied to Hollywood he would almost certainly have been unable to adjust to changing economic and social conditions. Hollywood was still a base, a home to which he could always come back with pleasure, but he could now range freely, making films in many countries and not labelled 'Hollywood: class of 1934'. His next film for instance was an Ealing comedy made in Britain called *The Love Lottery* (1953), directed by Charles Crichton.

The range of his roles was widening and in *Happy Ever After* (1954), directed by Mario Zampi, another British film, called *Tonight's the Night* in the United States, he played a thoroughly unpleasant character: an Irish landowner and more or less the villain of the piece.

Neither *The Love Lottery* nor *Happy Ever After* were successes and it has to be said that Niven was not a convincing villain.

The London *Evening News* lamented that he seemed 'most unhappy in the part,' a view echoed in the United States by the *Saturday Review*: 'Niven is wasted in this unsympathetic role.'

Carrington V.C. (1954) (*Court Martial* in the United States) was a reversion to type. Niven began to feel he would never get out of uniform – on the screen or off it he had worn military uniforms from almost every period in British history. There was no doubt about it, they did seem to suit him. He was being too modest when he wrote: 'For someone who made such a hash of his service experience, it's incongruous that I should have been in and out of uniform so many times.'

Directed by Anthony Asquith, *Carrington V.C.* told the story of Major Carrington, owed money by the War Office, oppressed by a collapsing marriage and court-martialled because, despite warning, he took some of what was owed him from the Battery safe.

Notwithstanding a certain stagebound clumsiness in the direction of the film, it was Niven's best role in a long time. Said the *Observer*: 'Niven, one should remember, has not always been a light comedian, many people will be glad to re-encounter the graver actor of *The Dawn Patrol*.'

Such plaudits were welcome, but Niven still felt obliged to take what was offered to him. *The King's Thief* (1955), directed by Robert Z. Leonard, a piece of superficial, period hokum, was followed by *The Birds and the Bees* (1956) directed by Norman Taurog, a tedious remake of Preston Sturges's *The Lady Eve* (1941). Both these, though, were in Hollywood, but it was a Hollywood that had changed immeasurably.

Mike Todd was a product of the old Hollywood. He would not have been out of place at a cigar-chomping convention of moguls of the old school: Goldwyn, Zanuck, Warner. He was larger than life, bursting with ideas and radiating razzmatazz. When he did things they had to be worth doing, like marrying Elizabeth Taylor. He chose David

Opposite above: Bette Davis, centre, readies herself for a movie stars' 'excuse me'.
Opposite below: Bette Davis joins Frances Langford and Edward G. Robinson in a radio broadcast. Langford was a popular band singer who appeared in a number of light musicals, including Too Many Girls *(1940),* Swing it, Soldier *(1941) and* The Girl Rush *(1944). She appeared as herself in* The Glenn Miller Story *(1954).*

Niven to play the lead in *Around the World in Eighty Days* (1956), directed by Michael Anderson and Kevin McClory.

Adapted from the novel by Jules Verne, the story tells how Phileas Fogg (Niven) makes a bet that he can circle the globe in eighty days. It was produced on an epic scale and was a wonderful excuse to introduce a whole range of guest stars in cameo roles. Marlene Dietrich, Noël Coward, Frank Sinatra, Ronald Colman, Buster Keaton, Shirley MacLaine, all had an opportunity of doing their party piece. Making the film was, as Niven said, 'pure fantasy'. It was self-indulgent but irresistible.

Somehow or other the flamboyant Todd managed to raise the millions to finance the film, although creditors, lawyers, accountants pursued him relentlessly throughout the making of the film.

Elizabeth Taylor watches Montgomery Clift while he adjusts the moustache he wore in sequences of Raintree County *(1958).*

The ballyhoo surrounding the whole operation was spectacular and the statistics much quoted: the most stars ever brought together for one film (50); the most people ever photographed on world-wide location (68,984 in thirteen different countries); the most miles travelled to make a film (4 million air passenger miles) – it was meant to impress and it did.

For 1956 it was the movie of the year and as one might have predicted it won the Oscar for best movie. Well, it had cost six million dollars. . . . Truth to tell, seeing it again today, it strikes one as a rather ponderous film, a celebration of the overblown which never quite turns a trot into a gallop. Niven, however, bubbled above it all

David Niven with Shirley MacLaine during the filming of Ask Any Girl *(1959), directed by Charles Walters. MacLaine's bubbly performance as a naïve out-of-towner in New York won her the Silver Bear as the 'best foreign actress' at the 1959 Berlin Film Festival.*

to win the kind of acclaim which made him wonder just what he had done to deserve it all.

The *Manchester Guardian* said: 'David Niven's quite essentially English gentleman is never in any danger of disappearing: he dominates even this gigantic screen with as fine a performance as he has given us for many a long year.'

Niven himself thought it was essentially Mike Todd's movie, and that is how it should be remembered. 'Mike was of the old breed of tycoon – but nicer than most. He put his – or, rather, other people's – money where his mouth was. His early death was tragic, but then his death at any time would have been tragic. He was so very much *alive!*'

Where to go next. It seemed impossible to plan a career, it was just a case of making dozens of movies in the hope that every tenth one would be a success. It is a tribute to the great affection Niven's public now had for him that his career survived another string of embarrassingly bad films.

Said the London *Daily Sketch* of his performance in *The Little Hut* (1957), directed by Mark Robson, in which he co-starred with Ava Gardner and Stewart Granger: 'David Niven – the one saving grace.' One effort Niven made to take control of his career was to form, with Charles Boyer and Dick Powell, the Four Star Playhouse, a television company.

Then in 1958 came *Separate Tables*, directed by Delbert Mann. It proved beyond all doubt that Niven could act when he wanted to and won him an Oscar. It showed that he had come a long way while, as he put it, 'learning and being paid for it'.

Written by the British playwright Terence Rattigan, it concentrates on a small private hotel in an English seaside resort populated by lonely, unhappy long-term guests. Niven's role was that of an old-school-tie character, Major Pollack, befriended by a mother-dominated Deborah Kerr. Pollack is revealed to be neither a major nor the upright, above-board man he pretends to be, and is arrested for molesting women in a cinema.

What Niven was doing here, with some courage, was displaying the other side of the usual character he played. The English gentleman he enjoyed being in real life and which had stood him in such good stead throughout his movie career might be, he teased, just a mask. In his performance in *Separate Tables* he revealed the man who wanted to belong yet who must always remain an outsider.

The London *Daily Herald* said of Niven: 'At the age of 48, he joins the select ranks of the screen masters.' The New York film critics presented their annual award to him, and then came the Oscar. It was received by him in a typically Niven manner. As he wrote: 'Such was my haste to get on that stage that I tripped up the stairs and sprawled headlong...I thought the least I could do was to explain my precipitous entrance, so I said: "The reason I just fell down

David Niven with the Oscar he won for his performance as the bogus Major Pollack in Separate Tables *(1958).*

Left: With his adopted daughters Fiona (left) and Christina.
Below left: As Corporal Miller, the explosives expert, in Carl Foreman's The Guns of Navarone (1961).
Below right: The doting father.

Above left: Relaxing with Gregory Peck on location for The Guns of Navarone. *Above: With Peter Sellers, in 1971.*

was . . .'' I had intended to continue ''because I was so loaded with good luck charms that I was top heavy . . .'' Unfortunately, I made an idiot pause after the word ''loaded'' . . . So I said no more on the subject, thereby establishing myself as the first self-confessed drunk to win the Academy Award.'

In his book *The Moon's a Balloon*, Niven describes the Oscar presentation but is notably reticent on the matter of actually performing the role of Major Pollack. The *Sunday Times* said of him: 'David Niven's Major with his loping military gait, the timing of his peppery officer's jargon, and the bland, faintly shadowed stare of a man whose life is a lie, is beautifully characterised.'

What Niven told me about it was: 'It was a part that took a lot out of me. I understood that kind of loneliness but I had not been particularly lonely.'

I believe that Niven's own childhood was training enough for the part of Major Pollack. Much of the time the young Niven had had to pretend that all was well when all was far from well. In this rather mechanical play Niven found the role he had spent half a lifetime learning to play.

Whatever the reason, it is a remarkable screen portrayal, well deserving of an Oscar; but, if that award meant that the film world was now to be his oyster, there were certainly no pearls contained therein. Once again Niven chose films which were undistinguished; not disreputable but hardly good enough for him. They all bore a label 'made in Hollywood' but it was by now ersatz Hollywood, a pale reflection of the glittering, crudely creative place it had once been.

Niven was happier now. He had status, an Oscar to prove to himself he could act if he were asked and a family including two adopted daughters. It was only sad that there seemed no one around prepared to ask Niven to act. He drifted through bad films without effort, a sleep-walker lacking the ambition to search out the film that could win him another Oscar.

In 1961, though he got a part in *The Guns of Navarone*, directed by J. Lee-Thompson, a hugely expensive wartime epic which boasted such luminaries as Gregory Peck and Anthony Quinn. The story, from a novel by Alistair MacLean, tells how a small group of Allied saboteurs infiltrate the island of Navarone to destroy the mighty guns which threaten what is described as 'a vital Allied operation'. It was all hyped-up *Boys' Own Paper* stuff, with Niven this time playing out of the officer-class: Corporal Miller.

The writer and co-producer Carl Foreman wrote: 'David is, of course, a pleasure to work with, a producer and director's delight, supremely co-operative, always cheerful, always prepared, a ripple-maker of tremendous ingenuity and, of course, one of the great raconteurs of all time.'

Which is the kind of thing you would expect a producer to say in public about his star, but Foreman went on to comment on Niven's tenacity, his refusal to give in. 'He is, moreover, a very brave man. I shall never forget how he literally dragged himself from a sick bed, barely recovered from a near-fatal blood disease, and insisted on completing a vital scene which, by holding up the completion of the film, was threatening a financial disaster to the distributors, Columbia Pictures. The consequences to David would have been more serious as well as conclusive.'

It was, of course, for David Niven a question of not letting the side or the school down.

The Guns of Navarone was, though, rather overshadowed by the barrage of publicity which had preceded it, although the London *Sunday Telegraph* thought it was all 'Absolutely superlative of its sort, right up to the very end when we are treated to what must be the most ear-shattering bang in the whole history of the sound film.'

Niven's own reviews were not so ecstatic, *The Observer* lamenting that he was in this movie an other-ranker, commented: 'Like all male British stars David Niven has an inescapable military rank and his is not a pip less than second lieutenant!

'The excuse that he refused a commission because he wanted to avoid the responsibility for killing people is scarcely acceptable

With an old friend, Prince Rainier.

Above left: Sharing a joke with Prince Rainier's son, Albert, at a Monte Carlo casino. When David Niven left Hollywood to settle in Europe, the Rainiers became his favourite neighbours. Above right and left: With Princess Grace, formerly the film star Grace Kelly. Beautiful, intelligent and oozing class, she was superb as the cool Hitchcock heroine offering Cary Grant a choice of breast or leg in To Catch a Thief (1955). The film's Monte Carlo background became her home after she married Rainier in 1956, following her final film, High Society (1956). She died tragically in a car accident in 1982.

when the character has such lip-clenching and absolutely officer-like lines of determination around the jaw.'

Niven set his own jaw and, privately, thought that the film and his role were good ones. Certainly, it was a huge box-office success and it reinforced him as an international star. He still enjoyed making films in Hollywood because 'everything is so streamlined from the unions to the production itself', but more and more he made films elsewhere. Symbolically, he set up a new home in Switzerland, the country of Hollywood exiles, where old friends like the Chaplins made him very welcome.

Sad to say, the films he was making in the 1960s until his death in 1983 are not on any critic's list of best movies. He had another go at an old-style historical epic with *55 Days at Peking* (1963), produced by Samuel Bronston and directed by Nicholas Ray and Andrew Marton. Then there was *The Pink Panther* (1964), directed by Blake Edwards, which was hardly any kind of test for Niven, although it gave Peter Sellers as Inspector Clouseau a minor role which he brilliantly expanded into a major one, and a deservedly popular series of comedies.

Bedtime Story in 1964, directed by Ralph Levy, improbably teamed Niven with Marlon Brando. It proved to be a film of which the London *Daily Express* could say: 'The most vulgar and embarrassing film of the year', but concluded that 'David Niven . . . stands quietly by garnering all the chuckles with subtle skill while Brando makes a monkey of himself.'

There followed *Lady L* (1965) for Peter Ustinov and the *Eye of the Devil* (1967), directed by J. Lee-Thompson, which bizarrely cast Niven as a Chief Satanist. However, probably the most disastrous movie of this period was the expensive fiasco *Casino Royale* (1967), a spoof James Bond of quite irredeemable silliness which was directed by John Huston, Ken Hughes, Val Guest, Robert Parrish, Joe McGrath and Richard Talmadge.

Niven played a retired Sir James Bond and the London *Sunday Telegraph* said: 'David Niven stays scrupulous to the end, but in Peter Sellers, Woody Allen, Orson Welles, Deborah Kerr we see symptoms of the self-cherishing which presumes audiences to be comprised entirely of autograph hunters.'

The films he made slid rapidly downhill. Bad became worse: the worst was *The Statue* (1970), directed by Rod Amateau, a story which featured a statue of Niven with a penis very obviously not his own.

So why take such films? 'I like to be with mates.' Niven has said, and it is interesting to note how the names of his friends crop up again and again. When separated from them, though, and made to work in a less cozy atmosphere, he quite clearly was capable of achieving something very much more interesting. In 1972, for example, he made *King, Queen, Knave*, based on the novel by

Edward G. Robinson in his Hollywood home about the time he made I Loved a Woman *(1933) with Kay Francis. Three years earlier his performance as Little Rico, the Al-Capone-like gang boss in* Little Caesar *(1930), had catapulted him to stardom. The Hopi Indian rug and the caricatures hint at the superb art collection he was to assemble in the 1930s and 1940s. The G. in the middle of his name stands for nothing – 'God only knows or gangsters', as he once ironically remarked.*

Above left: J. B. Priestley, producer Erich Pommer and Charles Laughton discuss a script rewrite during the filming of Hitchcock's Jamaica Inn (1939). Erich Pommer was an extremely influential figure in the German cinema of the 1920s, producing The Cabinet of Dr Caligari (1919), Doctor Mabuse (1922), Metropolis (1926) and The Blue Angel (1930).
Above right: A dapper David Niven on the ski slopes at Gstaad.
Left: The immortal W. C. Fields perched somewhat unsteadily on a penny farthing supported by an eager gaggle of Paramount starlets.

Nabokov. The film was directed by the talented Polish director Jerzy Skolimowski. In this bizarre black comedy Niven realized a marvellous portrait of a self-made tycoon which is among his best performances.

In contrast his next film was *Vampira* (1974), which his old friend Clive Donner directed. Ken Annadin was another old friend, and it was for him, in 1975, that Niven made *Paper Tiger*. In it, he played a character reminiscent of the Major Pollack in *Separate Tables*.

I reviewed it in the *Sunday Telegraph* and wrote: 'What saves it all from absolute tepidity is David Niven's portrayal . . . the wary eye beneath the forehead's corrugation tells us the man has lived life at second-hand but would hate to be thought of as second-rate. It is a satisfying example of combined star-quality and acting skill.'

I quote this review because Niven wrote thanking me for the kind words, but he personally had liked the film, commenting on the warmth of the story.

Writers in Hollywood.
Left: P. G. Wodehouse, supreme among British humorous writers.
David Niven appeared as Bertie Wooster in a Twentieth Century-Fox Wodehouse adaptation,
Thank You, Jeeves *(1936), with Arthur Treacher as the ineffable Jeeves.*

By 1976, David Niven had severed practically all his Hollywood connections. He had virtually retired to Switzerland, only making the occasional movie such as the detective jape *Murder by Death* (1976), directed by Robert Moore, and a film for Disney, *Candleshoe* (1977), directed by Norman Tokar.

Of course, a professional actor like Niven never really retires and he was always waiting for the 'right' role. As Dilys Powell wrote in the *Sunday Times*: 'I wish only that someone could find the perfect role for Mr Niven. A Dickens character perhaps? Something out of Thackeray or Meredith. . . . He is an actor far more delicate, far more easily damaged by wrong treatment in the medium than his insouciant air might suggest. I can't help feeling that, lying around somewhere, there is a small masterpiece for David Niven.'

That small masterpiece never came along. But maybe it was replaced by his role in life itself. It was by now acknowledged that he had a unique place in people's affections and was cherished as, among other things, a brilliant raconteur. His memories of Hollywood were devoured eagerly by film fans the world over and his career as a whole added up to much more than its parts. Certainly a film of his Hollywood days would be an entertaining one. 'Every film was touted as a masterpiece', he once told me, 'when it came out we wondered why it was so awful.'

Above left: J. B. Priestley in Hollywood with Buster Keaton. Priestley's autobiographical book Midnight on the Desert *(1937), paints a fascinating picture of Hollywood.*
Above right: Ernest Hemingway and Gary Cooper meet by chance outside a cinema in 1956. Cooper starred in A Farewell to Arms *(1932) and, at Hemingway's insistence, played Robert Jordan in* For Whom the Bell Tolls *(1943).*

181

Goodbye to Hollywood

I counted myself fortunate in being a friend of David Niven's. Nothing extraordinary about that; he liked writers, and journalists, which is why the success of his books, *The Moon's a Balloon* and *Bring on the Empty Horses*, so delighted him.

I met him first when I was writing for a movie magazine called *Picturegoer*; a very raw and nervous newcomer to London. Niven put me entirely at ease by making out that it was he who was nervous of being interviewed. Ever after that he would phone when in London; we would chat, sometimes meet. He was a delightful man and a remarkable story-teller.

He knew he was good at making friends. 'I like people,' he would say, but it was also, I think, a need in him to make people members of the large, loving family he himself would so like to have been part of as a child.

He loved reminiscing about the outrageous personalities of the Hollywood he knew so well and happily quoted *Sir Cedric Hardwicke*, who, in his book *A Victorian In Orbit*, wrote: 'I believe that God felt sorry for actors so he created Hollywood to give them a place in the sun and a swimming pool. The price they had to pay was to surrender their talent.'

He also enjoyed quoting two other descriptions which he felt summed up Hollywood: 'A place where you spend more than you

Below left: No Hollywood star's home is complete without a pool, and The Pink House was no exception.
Below right: Holding the fruit of a lifetime's experience, his two best-selling books, and the 1977 Coronet book award, given to authors who have sold over a million copies of one book.

Left: Holidaying at Beaulieu with Bing Crosby, 1960. A book written by one of Crosby's sons revealed that laid-back pipe-puffing old Bingle was a harsh disciplinarian as a father. Below: David Niven with his family at Gstaad.

make, on things you don't need, to impress people you don't like' and 'never have I seen so many unhappy men making a hundred thousand dollars a year.'

Well, Niven liked people and he carefully hid whatever unhappiness he felt behind an attractive mask of self-mockery and genuine modesty. So, when he died on 29 July 1983, of the motor neurone disease which had been wasting his body so remorselessly over the years, a terrible fate for a man who prided himself on keeping so fit and healthy, hundreds of thousands of people grieved, for David Niven had made his audience his friends. There are too few people bringing laughter and light into the world as it is, to spare one with his joy in life.

He died a rich man, at the age of seventy-three, rich in money but richer in the affection he had earned after appearing in nearly a hundred films. David Niven's Hollywood has now vanished into thin air, but our continuing delight in it, revealed in the tremendous popularity of his two volumes of autobiography, amused Niven towards the end of his life. Perhaps our delight in the Hollywood of the thirties and forties reflects our nostalgia for a brash innocence that, in a strange way, David Niven shared.

The great Hollywood stars were also human beings who were puzzled by their fame and feared its disappearance. Most of them were not without a shrewd sense of their own worth: they knew it was all illusion and would enjoy reminding each other of the success of the confidence trick. The great screen-lover would click his false teeth in

Above left: Niven toying with Ginger Rogers in Bachelor Mother *(1939), directed at RKO by Garson Kanin. Norman Krasna's snappy screenplay gave Niven a chance to display his skill as a light comedian, playing a characteristically debonair, dissolute playboy.*
Above right: With Loretta Young in Eternally Yours *(1939), directed by Tay Garnett, in which Niven played an illusionist, The Great Arturo.*

his mistress's face. But it was not a fraud. Television has revealed the sheer 'watchability' of the stars and the films they appeared in. The Hollywood heritage that we are heirs to still dazzles and delights us. Through David Niven's career we can recapture a little of what it was like to start from almost the bottom and, through struggle and hard work and luck, reach that indefinable status we call 'a star'.

On 27 October 1983, a Memorial Service was held for David Niven in London at St Martin-in-the-Fields. John Mortimer, the distinguished author and playwright and an old friend of Niven's spoke of 'our joy in knowing a man who gave us so much happiness . . . He liked, above all things, to bring his friends together . . . So we are all his friends, those lucky enough to have known him, to have evenings of laughter or days of work shared and enjoyed to treasure, and those millions who came to love him through his films and his writing.'

Mortimer quoted what Ernst Lubitsch had said to Niven: 'Nobody should try and play comedy unless they have a circus going on inside.' Said John Mortimer: 'Perhaps that was the secret of David's style. He seemed so elegant and cool, he was so handsome and well dressed, but inside the band was forever striking up, the children were clapping with delight and the clowns were always about to be brought on.'

Below left: A film from the 1980s, Ménage à Trois, *also released as* Better Late than Never *(1983), which starred Maggie Smith, Art Karney and Kimberley Partridge.*
Below right: The quintessential Niven, elegant and charming and, as so often in his career marooned in an indifferent film. This one was Sam Goldwyn's Enchantment *(1948).*

Niven could even make a joke about his desperate illness. When his voice was almost gone he said to Mortimer: 'Perhaps it's because I've talked too much all my life that this has got me now.'

David Niven liked to tell of the custom in some Swiss villages of darkening the lights when one of their men was killed on the mountains. I would like to think that the already dimmed lights of modern Hollywood flickered when Niven died. One thing is certain: as long as Hollywood is remembered – the star of David Niven will go on shining brightly.

Romancing Merle Oberon in Beloved Enemy *(1936).*

Afterword by David Niven Jr

Fortunately, many people are well equipped to write about the David Niven they knew as a man, writer, actor and friend. Only four people knew him as a father and, as the oldest, I naturally knew him the longest.

Notwithstanding his busy schedules, he always had plenty of time for each of us. We all received his support and guidance for whatever endeavours we wished to pursue. He never insisted any of us be 'The' Best . . . only to do 'Our' Best.

He instilled in us the value of family unity, the importance of loyalty, humility and honesty.

As a father he showed no favouritism and was always there whenever we needed him. There were times when he was 'Father', 'Older Brother', yet always 'Friend'.

He loved us all very very much and I only hope we gave him as much love and pleasure as he gave us. In spite of the fact that we won't see him again, he will always be in our hearts and we will miss him tremendously.

David Niven Jr.

Niven with David Niven Jr.

David Niven's Films

Without Regret 1935
Barbary Coast 1935
A Feather in Her Hat 1935
Splendor 1935
Rose Marie 1936
Palm Springs 1936
Thank You, Jeeves 1936
Dodsworth 1936
The Charge of the Light Brigade 1936
Beloved Enemy 1936
We Have Our Moments 1937
The Prisoner of Zenda 1937
Dinner at the Ritz 1937
Bluebeard's Eighth Wife 1938
Four Men and a Prayer 1938
Three Blind Mice 1938
The Dawn Patrol 1938
Wuthering Heights 1939
Bachelor Mother 1939
Eternally Yours 1939
The Real Glory 1939
Raffles 1939
The First of the Few 1942
The Way Ahead 1944
A Matter of Life and Death 1946
The Perfect Marriage 1946
Magnificent Doll 1946
The Other Love 1947
The Bishop's Wife 1947
Bonnie Prince Charlie 1948
Enchantment 1948
A Kiss in the Dark 1949
The Elusive Pimpernel 1949
A Kiss for Corliss 1949
The Toast of New Orleans 1950
Happy Go Lovely 1950
Soldiers Three 1951
The Lady Says No! 1951
Appointment With Venus 1951
The Moon is Blue 1953
The Love Lottery 1953
Happy Ever After 1954
Carrington V.C. 1954
The King's Thief 1955

The Birds and the Bees 1956
Around the World in Eighty Days 1956
The Little Hut 1956
The Silken Affair 1956
Oh Men! Oh Women! 1957
My Man Godfrey 1957
Bonjour Tristesse 1957
Separate Tables 1958
Ask Any Girl 1959
Happy Anniversary 1959
Please Don't Eat the Daisies 1960
The Guns of Navarone 1961
The Best of Enemies 1961
The Captive City 1962
The Road to Hong Kong 1962
Guns of Darkness 1962
55 Days at Peking 1963
The Pink Panther 1964
Bedtime Story 1964
Lady L 1965
Where the Spies Are 1965
Eye of the Devil 1967
Casino Royale 1967
Prudence and the Pill 1968
The Impossible Years 1968
Before Winter Comes 1969
The Brain 1969
The Extraordinary Seaman 1969
The Statue 1970
King, Queen, Knave 1972
Vampira 1974
Paper Tiger 1975
No Deposit No Return 1976
Murder by Death 1976
Candleshoe 1977
Death on the Nile 1978
Escape to Athena 1979
A Man Called Intrepid 1979
A Nightingale Sang in Berkeley Square 1979
Rough Cut 1980
The Sea Wolves 1980
Trail of the Pink Panther 1982
Ménage à Trois 1983
Curse of the Pink Panther 1983

Acknowledgments

The author and publishers would like to thank Hamish Hamilton for permission to quote from *The Moon's a Balloon* and *Bring on the Empty Horses*; and Viking Penguin Inc. for permission to quote from *Memo from David O. Selznick* by Rudy Behlemer.

The author and publishers are also grateful to the following for permission to reproduce photographs on the pages indicated:

Barnaby's 60, 68, 78, 86, 87, 126; BBC Hulton Picture Library 11, 13 above, 14, 16 below, 17, 26, 33 above, 34, 35 right, 36, 37, 38, 39, 40, 41, 43 right, 44, 45, 46, 47, 48, 50, 51, 53, 54, 55 below right, 56, 57 left, 58, 59, 61, 62 below, 63, 65, 69 below right, 71, 73 right, 75, 82, 83 above left, 84, 88, 89, 91 left, 94, 95, 97, 98, 101 above and below left, 102, 103, 104 below, 105, 108, 109, 112 below left, 113 above and below left, 115, 116, 118, 119, 123, 124, 125, 127, 131, 134, 141, 144 above, 146 below left, 147, 152, 155, 159, 164 above right and below, 168, 178, 179 above left and below, 180; Camera Press 144 below, 145, 170, 174 above, 175 left, 187; Culver Pictures Inc. 72, 96, 129, 136, 150 above left and below, 162; Kobal Collection 2, 7, 12, 13 below, 15, 16 above, 18, 19, 20, 21, 27, 28, 32, 33 below, 42–3, 49, 55 above and below left, 57 right, 62 above, 64, 69 below left, 73 left, 76, 77, 83 below, 90, 91 above right and below, 92, 93, 99, 100, 101 below right, 104 above, 106, 107, 111, 112 above right, 113 below right, 114, 117, 121, 128 right, 132, 137, 143, 149, 153, 160, 167 left, 184, 185 right, 186; London Express News and Feature Services 165; Memory Shop 120, 150 above right, 151, 157 below left and right, 171, 174 below left, 179 above right; Popperfoto 31, 69 above, 163, 167 right; Courtesy J.B. Priestley 181 left; Private Collection 24, 25, 35 left, 67, 74, 81, 83 above right, 85, 112 above left and below right, 128 left, 133, 135, 138, 142, 146 above and below right, 148, 154, 157 above left, 158, 161, 164 above left, 177 below, 181 right; Rex Features 9, 82 right, 174 right, 176, 177 above left and right, 182, 183, 185 left; Syndication International 10, 22, 29, 156, 166, 175 right; Topham Picture Library 173.

If in any case the acknowledgment proves to be inadequate the publishers apologize. In no case is such inadequacy intentional, and if any owner of copyright who has remained untraced will communicate with the publishers, the required acknowledgment will be made in future editions of the book.

Index